THE FRIENDSHIP FORMULA

THE FRIENDSHIP FORMULA

HOW TO SAY GOODBYE TO LONELINESS AND DISCOVER DEEPER CONNECTION

KYLER SHUMWAY, MA

TABLE OF CONTENTS

FOREWORD

Let me tell you a story.

When I took the stage at TEDxBend 2018, I wanted to share a simple message. I wanted people to know that no matter what, they deserved friendship, and that no matter what, they had the ability to change someone else's life through the decision to be a friend.

My message was simple, but the response was profound. The stories of friendship that I shared on stage moved the audience deeply, and a crowd of thousands jumped to their feet as I took my final bow.

But the greatest story of friendship that day was about to unfold off-stage. As I emerged from the speakers' area, I was engulfed in a hug by my best friend, who had driven hours to support me during my big day. He praised me on my speech, pride brimming in his eyes, and then surprised me with this gigantic bag of gifts of congrats.

In it, were all the little things that I loved. There was a gift card to my favorite restaurant, a bag of my favorite candy, a T-shirt with the perfect reference to an inside joke, and so much more. In choosing all these things that I loved, my best friend let me know that *I* was loved – that he knew me deeply, and that my happiness was so important to him that he took the time to painstakingly create an incredible bag of delight just for me.

Let me tell you another story.

For most of my life, I was the scrawniest kid you would ever meet. In high school, a kid in my PE classes nicknamed me "huesos" (bones) because I was made of skin, bones, but no muscles. I couldn't even be angry – it was an accurate nickname!

But that changed when I met my best friend. I noticed his frequent gym visits and asked him to rate his ability to teach me how to dead-lift on a scale of 1-10. When he replied "11!" I knew I had found my perfect workout partner.

Through his patient coaching, I started to be comfortable in the weight room. I added more and more weight, until one day I was ready to deadlift 300 pounds for the first time. We got someone to video tape it for future generations, and my friend cued up "Eye of the Tiger" as I bravely moved to kick the name "huesos" for good. I discovered that I possessed strength I never would have thought my-self capable of.

It was undeniably one of the proudest moments of my life. But if you watch the video, you'll notice something very odd. It's not the weird patterns of sweat drenching my shirt, or the awkward grimace my face made during my lift. In fact, it can be hard to miss if you're only focused on me.

However, if you look behind me, to where my best friend was stand-ing as he spotted me, you'd see it. When I lift the weight off the ground, his face lights up with absolute delight. And as I set the weight back down, he whoops and claps with joy. In fact, if you watch both us, it's clear that he is far more excited about my success than I am.

Why is that? Why is someone who could easily deadlift twice my record utterly delighted by my achievement? Why is it that his joy in my success is greater than my own?

There's only one explanation.

It's that my best friend loves me. Because the deepest core of friend-ship – the thing that we're all really searching for, if we're honest - is love. We all want friendships where we can be fully ourselves, and be accepted anyway. We all want friendships where you that both of you will have each other's back no matter what. We all want friend-ships that are built on a bedrock foundation of love. And Kyler has discovered the formula to build those friendships.

That's right – As you've probably guessed, my best friend is Kyler Shumway, the author of the book that you hold in your hands. I'm so glad you're going to have the opportunity to learn from him.

I've read dozens of books on social skills, relationships, and connection. I've traveled to conferences around the country where amazing speakers discuss the best ways to form connections. And yet I've never met someone with the same profound wisdom towards friendship as Kyler.

Kyler Shumway understands what it means to be a friend – understands what it takes to build a friendship that satisfies you to the core and that is built to last a lifetime. The book that you hold in your hands will teach you to do the same. Bon voyage.

—Daniel Wendler, M.A.
Author of *ImproveYourSocialSkills.com*
TEDxBend 2018 Speaker "What Being Autistic Taught Me About Being Human"

INTRODUCTION

Contrary to popular opinion, friendship is not a noun.

Friendship is a verb, a process, an art.

Friendship is the jovial dance of belonging. It is the epic journey of finding the connection and love that comes with having friends. It is the joining together of cheese and jalapeno to add some zest to our brief mortal fiesta.

We are hardwired for relationship. We work and play better when we do it together. We crave spaces of belonging for our very survival.

Despite our interconnected nature, we face a loneliness epidemic.

A study from 2015 published in *Perspectives on Psychological Science* suggested that social disconnection may actually be killing us – with an increased risk of death at 26% for reported loneliness and 29% for social isolation regardless of age, socioeconomic status, and current health issues.

No wonder so many of us find ourselves in a frantic search for connection.

The problem is, too many people try to learn how to "make friends" rather than learn how to be better at friendship. We invest so much time and energy trying to figure out how to get more fish, without really learning about how to be better fishermen. Friendship is not about catching the prize of connection, friendship is the means to finding it.

Folks, this is what my book is all about.

The year was 2018. The place, TEDx Bend Oregon. I had front row seats as my best friend in the whole wide world, Daniel Wendler, delivered his speech to thousands of eager listeners.

His stories of rejection, fear, and being "invisible" wrought images of intense pain and interpersonal suffering all too common in modern society – myself included. After nearly a decade of working in hospitals, assisted-living facilities, and schools I have learned just what an epidemic loneliness has become. And yet, many of us who feel alone are not alone.

Dan's solution to the suffering of loneliness was simple: be the friend.

"There's an old Jewish parable, called the parable of the long spoons. And it says that heaven and hell are the exact same place. Everyone is seated around a big table with a huge pot of delicious soup, and each person has a really long spoon. And in hell, everyone is starving because there's just no way to bring these long spoons to your mouth without spilling all of the soup. But in heaven, everyone is full and happy because they feed each other and are fed in return."

By being the friend for someone else, you can make the world a bit more like heaven. Overwhelmed with manly tears of intense joy, I whooped and joined the crowd in a standing ovation for this powerful message – one that I now raise as a banner for my book. Dan's talk was powerful for me, and not just because he is my best friend. His message of belonging by creating space for belonging spoke to something within me, something I believe all of us share.

As a therapist, I see people on their very worst days, wracked with thoughts of suicide, drunk with sorrow, lost in their pain. After you meet a few hundred of these tortured souls, you start to notice patterns. Loneliness reigned supreme as time after time I met with those without anyone to care for them.

Human connection is a fundamental need, and I want to help people find it. Each of us is worthy of belonging. Each of us deserves to feel loved. And, each of us can provide those things for someone else.

The desire to be seen and known by others has long been lumped in a dirty pile with narcissism and greed. And yet, many of us feel the starvation of loneliness and fear of being forgotten. Friendship is not a luxury set upon the peaks of Maslow's pyramid, it is a foundational need for survival. From birth, we are taught to feed and water ourselves, yet we do not always learn how to connect with one another.

If you Google "how to make friends," you will find thousands of self-help books on conversation tactics, seduction and manipulation, relationship secrets, and how to be more charismatic. Many of those books are helpful, and some of them will help you learn how to make friends. Yet, few of them speak to the powerful psychosocial mechanisms behind friendship, and how you can make new friends simply by doing what my buddy Dan suggests – be the friend.

The Friendship Formula is not just a self-help book. This is an other-help book, one that will bring you to a place of deeper understanding, awareness, and capacity to provide a space of belonging. In turn, you will begin to reap the benefits of connection and feel the same sense of trust and belonging that I share with my friends. Let us then make the world a bit more like heaven by bringing connection to one another.

The Friendship Formula is simple:

The Art of Friendship = Looking Inward +
Looking Outward + Looking In Between

I based this structure on Interpersonal Psychology and Cognitive Behavioral concepts used by licensed clinicians to provide you with a holistic understanding of relationships. In other words, this is the formula that the pros use. This book is also chock full of scientific evidence for why *The Friendship Formula* can help you meet your goals. Here is how it works.

Looking Inward is all about learning to take care of yourself and maximize your capacity for friendship. This section is designed to help you identify the unique aspects of your needs and personality that will improve your ability to be a better friend.

Looking Outward is all about using your insights, learning the dos and don'ts of relationship, and reaching out. This is about taking care of others, much like a gardener learns to use his tools to foster growth, in the quest to build healthy, meaningful relationships.

Looking In Between provides a framework for understanding relationships and how to keep a connection happy and healthy. This is about learning how to take care of the relationship itself as if the friendship had a life of its own.

Just like fishing, skiing, cooking, and writing, friendship is a skill that can be mastered. I believe with all my heart that learning how to be a better friend will bring you closer to meaningful and lasting friendship, and I am proud to join you on this journey.

PART I
LOOKING INWARD

When I said the final goodbye to my childhood friend, I felt nothing.

I was fourteen years old. My parents were moving our family across the state, close to nine hours away, and it was the last time my friend and I were going to hang out. Our families met through church, and we quickly bonded over video games and our obsession with *The Lord of the Rings*. We stayed up all night on that final get together, playing Halo 2, drinking Mountain Dew, and chomping on frozen cookie dough bites.

When the sun came up, and my dad arrived to take me home, my friend began to cry. My body was numb, I couldn't even think straight.

"Bye, Kyler. I am going to miss you a lot. Do you think you will come back to visit?"

I just looked at him. Nothing. What the heck was going on with me?

"Um…" I said, "No, I don't think so."

And then I got in my dad's pickup truck, and I felt nothing.

I could have totally called him, played more video games online with him, anything.

But, I didn't.

In fact, I didn't make another friend for an entire decade. And it wasn't until I began studying as a psychologist that I realized what had happened.

Something inside of me, something about the way I relate with others, affected my capacity for friendship. It took looking inward and understanding myself to take that next step, reach out, and build a new relationship. This is what Part 1 is all about.

Here's a difficult question. If today you were to meet that person, the one who would be your best friend forever, would they want to be friends with you? This question comes from the idea of the "soulmate" – that person who was placed on this planet for you and you for them. Some churches use this as a motivational tool to encourage us to better ourselves in preparation for a future spouse. Although I may not wholly believe in soulmates, I love the idea of preparing oneself for relationship. This, my friends, is what I hope this part of the book will do for you.

A famous psychologist and author named Carl Rogers once said that only when we fully accept ourselves are we able to change. Change must first come from a sort of self-recognition and willingness to come to terms with ourselves as perfectly imperfect. Preparing for friendship can be difficult, but the reward is well worth the investment.

So, what does it mean to "look inward?"

What does it mean to recognize and accept oneself?

What does it take to change?

CHAPTER 1
THE SEVEN DEADLY SCHEMAS

Unfurl a large blank scroll in your mind and stretch it across the table. This is your timeline, the story of your life.

To your left, we see your birth. To the right, we see you. At this moment, staring down at this book.

There is a lot of story between these points. You might have memories that stand out; birthday parties, the first days of school, that trip to the beach, that time you farted in a public elevator and tried to cover it with a cough. But we knew. We knew.

These memories come together to form what psychologists call "schemas," or foundational beliefs and feelings about yourself and about the world. Your life story is rich with memories of relationships. Some of those relationships were helpful and positive, while others were toxic. There may be significant gaps between these memories, where you felt invisible, disconnected and friendless. Imagine what it would be like if you tried to tell your story using only those relational memories. These are the building blocks of the schemas that shape your view of friendship.

Some of you may come to this book in a place of great pain, isolation, and rejection. You may have powerful schemas about yourself and others that make you feel hopeless when it comes to friendship. I know, I have some of those myself.

No matter how overwhelming these schemas feel, you have the power to find acceptance and belonging. I believe that with all my heart. This chapter is all about recognizing unhelpful relationship schemas, and learning how to challenge the beliefs that hold us back.

I give you... *The Seven Deadly Schemas.*

Schema #1: "I am not a social person"

Alas, many of us carry this schema around with us. We work up the courage to go to a party, only to sit by the chip bowl avoiding eye contact with others. This belief is a self-fulfilling prophecy, isn't it? We sit back and watch the social people engage with one another while we focus on eating snacks in comfort.

And that's the problem. The comfort.

Those of us who agree with this schema tend to feel uncomfortable when they act socially. There seems to be a powerful emotion that comes with that discomfort – fear. And it happens even in the smallest of small talks. We are afraid of messing up and saying something stupid. We are afraid of what the other person thinks of us. We are scared that they are going to notice how anxious and uncomfortable we feel. As soon as the conversation ends, we breathe a sigh of relief and return to our chip bowl.

The brain is very good at learning what feels unsafe. Although most social interactions are not life-threatening, your mind is trying to get you back to that chip bowl, that safe haven. Each time we avoid the discomfort our brains learn to reinforce the avoidant behavior. "Stay by the bowl..." your brain rattles, "you are not a social person."

So, how do you challenge this schema?

It's simple, but easier said than done. You have to lean into the discomfort. You have to talk back to your brain and tell it why you want to be social; give it a reason to push through the pain. Sometimes, you can try adding something to the schema. "I am not a social person, **but I want to try and make a new friend today.**" I use this all the time when I need to motivate myself to do a workout. My body will screech "I don't want to lift weights today," and I will add *"but I want to get stronger and be healthy."* And just like with working out, challenging a schema takes time and practice. It may be difficult at first, but I promise it gets easier.

Schema #2: "I just don't fit in"

This schema is tricky. One time, I accidentally walked into a women's bathroom. And, at least last time I checked, I am not a woman. As soon as I realized that I did not fit in, I quickly left. And I never went back to that McDonald's again.

Sometimes, we really do not fit in. This is another lesson that our brains are really good at learning, and it is an important skill to have. Otherwise, we might walk into the woods to try to join a pack of hungry wolves. The feeling of not fitting in keeps us safe from potential threats and keeps us in comfortable situations.

The problem is, this schema can grow into something much larger. We might feel like we do not fit in with others at all, that we do not deserve relationships, or that we are too alien and weird to connect with other people. Just like the schema of not being a social person, this schema is a self-fulfilling prophecy. The partner in crime of "not fitting in" is "others will not accept you." So why bother? Why waste your precious time and energy trying to be social, trying to fit in if you will only be met with rejection. In the great quest of making friends, you have decided instead to stay in your cozy house under the hill.

So, how do you kick this schema?

This one is all about risks. Every wager comes with odds, and in a way, every social interaction is a gamble. We cannot control what others might think or say, and so we cannot predict the social outcome. What odds might you give being rejected by others? Probably not one hundred percent, right? But that is how this schema makes us feel. We feel unacceptable, unlovable, and hopeless.

In a way, fishing is a bit like gambling. People wager their time and money to get out on the lake and try to catch a fish. Try. They might cast their line a hundred times with no luck. And yet, people keep fishing. As far as I know, people who fish do not start the day by saying "there's no way any fish will want to bite my lure, I should probably just stay home."

Take the risk.

Recognize that there is a risk of being rejected, of others not making space for you. And if you are rejected, that is okay. You can always fish again tomorrow.

Schema #3: "I am so awkward"

I hear this all the time in therapy sessions, and I tell it to myself sometimes. Just like the other schemas, this feeling of awkwardness has a purpose. Feeling awkward is the mind's way of alerting us that we may be doing something inappropriate or wrong. Think of it as a sort of internal radar that pings every time something out of place happens.

People on the autism spectrum or who identify as autistic tend to have trouble with this radar. They are not always able to pick up on social cues, which means they have to learn them manually. Nonetheless, autistic people can still have these same feelings of being awkward because of how others might treat them.

Sometimes the thought of being awkward is helpful. It helps regulate our behavior and keep us from doing something bizarre or dangerous, like biting someone just for fun. No, please don't do that. That would be awkward. And for the right reasons.

But mostly, the thought of being awkward keeps us from taking risks and being ourselves. We get so caught up in how we think our hair looks, how our words are coming out, and how that little bit of spit just flew out of our mouth, it distracts us from being fully present and in the moment.

Think about the last time you tried to talk to someone while they were distracted. Maybe they were talking and texting, or trying to make eye contact with someone else, or late for a meeting somewhere. It probably felt, well, a little awkward for you. This is what happens when we get caught up feeling awkward. We are not focused on the person we are talking to, we are focused on ourselves and all of our little imperfections.

The key to overcoming this schema comes in one word: acceptance. You have to radically accept that, unless you are a flawlessly designed social robot that communicates with perfection, you are going to be awkward sometimes. And that is okay. You can let yourself be a human being, foibles and all.

You are a complex creature, gifted with talents and flaws that make you interesting.

Have you ever thought about what makes superheroes so exciting? Superheroes are entertaining to watch because they come with great power - while also being vulnerable. Superhero shows would be far less attractive if the hero had no weaknesses, no areas for improvement. Imagine a hero that could never be killed or harmed and who could stop any enemy at any time. Although that hero may be impressive, their story would get boring after a while. There's no adventure when the outcome is certain, and the hero has no room to grow. This is why we love characters like Batman, who, despite having riches and gadgets and wicked black spandex, can still be hurt by bullets and mean words.

You are incredibly human, which makes you incredibly imperfect and incredibly valuable.

Schema #4: "I am boring"

When I was in the 3rd grade, I suddenly realized how boring I was.

Even with a weird name like "Kyler," people didn't seem to remember me for anything. I wasn't the cool kid, the smart kid, the pretty kid, or even the mean kid no one likes to be around. I was the invisible kid. And then one day, I came up with a brilliant solution to my problem: I decided to take on a British accent. The *Harry Potter* books and films were booming back then, and so I had plenty of exposure, and I was ready. "'Ello guvnor! 'Tis quite hot out t'day, yeah?"

What I wasn't ready for was the way people reacted. "What's wrong with you?" "Why are you talking like that?" "You're weird." Weird?

Wrong? I was trying to not be boring, but I did not like being those things. So, I went back to being the invisible kid.

The fear of boring-ness is seated right next to the fear of rejection. Perhaps worse, the fear of being boring is the fear that others will feel *nothing* towards us. How are we supposed to make new friends if others do not seem interested in spending times with us?

The trouble with being boring is it puts us at a nasty fork in the road. Option one, we keep being boring and avoid making a total doofus of ourselves. Option two, we try something new to try to be less boring. But, there is another option.

Imagine you are in a courtroom. There is a judge, two lawyers, and you. You have just been put on trial for the heinous crime of being boring. One lawyer is putting forth all of the evidence that you are, indeed, boring. The other lawyer is putting forth evidence to the contrary, anything that indicates that you are even the slightest bit interesting. What do you think these lawyers might say?

If you were to look at a chicken's egg, just a plain old white egg, you might say that it is boring. But if you look closely, you might notice that the shell is rough and textured. There might be a slight curve to the side of the egg that sets it apart from the others in the crate. Even this egg has something special. What makes you so sure that you are more boring than this little thing?

Each of us has a story to tell. Each of us has memories and experiences that make us who we are, and guess what? There are exactly zero people in this universe that are exactly like you. Think about it. If you had an identical clone, that clone would see the world through an entirely separate pair of eyes and form different ideas and interests.

And, even if you were totally boring, that doesn't mean you cannot be special. In the story of *The Little Prince*, a young boy encounters a fox. The fox asks the prince for deeper connection, to be "tamed" by the boy. The fox explains that without the connection, the boy is just like any other boy, and the fox is just like any other fox. When the two became friends, the boy said "He was only a fox like a hundred thousand other foxes. But I have made him my friend, and now he is unique in all the world."

Schema #5: "People don't want to make new friends"

This is our first schema that deals with others, rather than ourselves. You can almost hear the echoes of feeling left out and unwanted.

The harsh reality with this schema is that it is (mostly) true. Some people just do not want to make new friends. Some people are happy with their current circle of friendship. Some people believe one of their other schemas, and so they do not respond when others try to connect with them. And some people are just jerks. This is all part of the glorious existence we live in.

I know, it sucks.

But you know what, this schema is not entirely accurate. There have to be people out there who want to make friends, right? Look at you, reading this book! You must be one of those people. One of the good ones.

Just like with the schema of being awkward, we have to learn to accept this part of our society. Life is not all rainbows and tacos. But, sometimes we do get tacos, and sometimes the rainbows give a sendoff to the storm.

You are not alone. Mark Watney from *The Martian* was stranded on a distant planet. He was very much alone. But you are not. You, unlike Mark, have the distinct advantage of being on planet Earth – a place filled to the brim with lonely souls just like you. Do not give up so quickly, my friends. Intelligent life is out there.

Schema #6: "That person is too cool/pretty/smart/funny for me"

Ah yes, this is the Goldilocks schema. We want to be friends with people that interest us, but if they are *too* interesting, we think they are out of our league. In order for someone to be a good friend candidate, they have to be just right.

I remember the first time my friend Dan and I did anything together. This was before we were friends, and I was quite intimidated by him. He was always cracking good jokes in class, he drove a nice car, and not to mention that he was a published author and executive of the largest social skills platform I had ever heard of. During our second year of graduate school, Dan helped me get my first website set up, and so I decided to take him out to lunch.

When I was in grade school, I did not sit at the cool kids' table during lunch. I didn't even sit at the uncool kids' table. I used to skip lunch altogether, just to avoid being rejected or feeling awkward. Even as a grown man, I was terrified by the idea of taking *the* Daniel Wendler, the cool kid, to eat out at a local burger joint.

The funny thing is, I later found out that Dan felt the same way about me. He saw me as the jock, the D1 college athlete, the neuroscience whiz, the cool kid. Once we had the chance to get to know each other, the possibility of friendship emerged.

You see, cool kids need friends too. Sometimes the cool kids are the ones that feel the most insecure inside, and would gladly welcome your friendship. And, just as you look at others and think, "Wow, they are way too cool for me," there is a pretty good chance other people think that about you as well.

Schema #7: "I am not good at making friends"

I used to think I was really, really good at baking cookies. I used to pretend I was a hotshot chef, tossing ingredients across the counter, throwing the dough in the air like pizza, you know the drill. Don't judge me, I was eight. I would bake these peanut butter cookies for my parents and siblings all the time. Everyone would take one, smile, and say thank you as I happily skipped back to the kitchen to clean up.

And then one day, I caught my mom sneakily tossing a few of the freshly baked cookies into the trash. I was dumbfounded and obviously hurt, but my mom explained to me that the cookies were missing a few key ingredients... and almost always had eggshell bits inside. Although everyone wanted to be polite and take my cookies, I just was not very good at making them yet.

Just as Dr. Carl Rogers once said, only when we fully see and accept ourselves are we able to change. At first, I wanted to argue with my mom. Maybe she was just jealous that I could cook, too! Maybe she wanted us to eat healthier, but she didn't want to outright say that.

Or maybe, just maybe, I was not very good at making cookies.

Although Schema #7 might be somewhat irrational or blown out of proportion, it might also be a recognition of needed skill. In other words, it may feel very honest. This book is all about learning how to be a good friend, but the end goal remains the same. We want to be a good friend so that we can have good friends. And sometimes gaining friendship means we need to learn how to do friendship better.

So, I practiced. I asked for some coaching from my parents, I read actual recipes, and I got feedback after every batch. It took time, but I eventually got better at making cookies.

And you can, too.

The psychologist Dr. Carol Dweck is famous for her work regarding "The Growth Mindset." Having a growth mindset is all about focusing on learning and continuing to persevere. As we continue to work on being a good friend, we perfect our friendship recipe. We keep pushing forward, try new things, learn from and accept our shortcomings, and try again and again until we get it right.

You are taking the first step. Right here and now. By picking up this book, you have started your journey. And I am proud to be here with you.

Chapter Summary

Our first step in learning how to become a better friend involves a deep dive into our thoughts and feelings. Schemas are foundational beliefs that we develop to help understand ourselves and how the world works. Although some schemas are helpful, sometimes they inhibit our ability to attach with others and make new connections. This chapter highlights some of the most common detrimental schemas, the ones I call The Seven Deadly Schemas, which keep us from achieving our relational goals. When we carry schemas such as "I do not fit in" or "I am not a social person," we create self-fulfilling prophecies. Each of us can overcome these schemas by challenging our assumptions, taking new risks, and accepting our own human imperfections.

Questions to Ponder:

- What schemas do you carry with you? How have those affected your relational history?

- What gives you strength in the face of these schemas?

- Are there other schemas that get in your way? How might you face those?

CHAPTER 2
THE FIVE ESSENTIAL FOOD GROUPS OF FRIENDSHIP

I love video games, so very, very much.

Ever since I was little, I have been playing video games as a way to decompress and enjoy some good old-fashioned escapist fun.

One of my favorites is a game called *Don't Starve*. *Don't Starve* is all about, well, not starving. It is an open world survival game set in strange, Tim Burton-esque world where you have to keep your character alive by scavenging for food, avoiding dangerous predators, and maintaining their sanity.

When I first started playing, I just couldn't figure out how to keep myself well fed, healthy, and sane all at once. I spent loads of time wandering the world, looking for the perfect food that would meet all my needs at once.

In a way, relationships are a bit like *Don't Starve*.

Not all relationships are created equal. This is a good thing. Otherwise, your relationship with your mom would be the same as your relationship with your spouse, your barber, or even your pet goldfish. We get different things out of these relationships, which means different attachment needs are being met.

This chapter is all about understanding those needs.

Ask yourself this: what do you want out of friendship? Perhaps you hadn't thought of it that way before. Most of us experience loneliness and think that the solution is having a friend. The thing is, friends help us do so much more than placate our lonely feelings.

Think about food, for example. You know it, you love it, and you eat it. But food doesn't just make you feel less hungry. Each type of food helps meet a different nutritional need. Although the famous food pyramid is no longer advised, nutritionists still divide food into five primary groups. And so, just like the five essential food groups, here are the five essentials needs met through friendship:

Companionship

It is dangerous to go alone! As humans, we are hardwired for connection and relationship. We do not tend to feel great about being alone for long periods of time. Of course, there are outliers like the famed mountain men that live for years without seeing another human. But for the most part, each of us experiences a pull towards belonging.

My favorite illustration of this happens in the beloved British television series, *Dr. Who.*

The main protagonist, called The Doctor, is a time-traveling hero who uses his magnificent police box spaceship to solve the problems of the universe. But The Doctor doesn't travel alone. The Doctor always brings along a companion, a friend to share the experience of the wonders of space travel and adventure. The Doctor may not always need the help on a practical level, but it's still nice to have someone to spend time with.

You might feel a lack of companionship when you go to a school dance by yourself, or when you ask for a table for one at a restaurant, or when you try to ride a teeter-totter all by yourself. Companionship lets us know that we are not alone in this crazy universe of ours, and it helps us feel like we are part of someone else's story.

Fun

Fun is the sparkly pleasure and excitement that comes with the relationship. We need fun to inspire us, lift our spirits, and shake up the humdrum of everyday life. Friendships that bring us fun seem to be based on shared interests or activities; and yet, fun is more than just momentary pleasure. It's about creating memories.

You may feel a lack of fun in your life if you find yourself living in the routine, where weeks and months blur together in a grey haze. Our brains are quite good at storing memories, especially when those memories have a strong emotional valence. Life tends to hand us our fair share of painful, sad, and difficult memories, and so it is critical that we balance those with memories of goofy laughter and movie theater popcorn.

Empathy

Perhaps the best part of friendship is being able to share with one another, feel heard, and be understood. Friends help lift us up when we fail the big exam or lose a family member. They also cheer alongside us in our moments of victory and share our pride.

Empathy meets a deep, psychological need. No matter how successful we are or accomplished we might be, it matters less when we feel unseen. No matter how hurt we feel or downtrodden we might be, it feels worse when no one else gets it.

Empathy is the greatest of all human superpowers. If only we were better at giving it to one other.

People who do not experience much empathy in their relationships may begin to feel jaded, misunderstood, or isolated. This lack of nourishment can lead to resignation about relationships and feelings of spite towards others. Some of you might feel this way, and for that I am so deeply sorry. You may be in a frightening and disconnected place. But do not give up. There are people out there who care about you and want to understand your story. You matter very much.

Assistance

Sometimes, we just need a ride to the airport.

Friends can also help meet some of our practical needs. They might take notes for you while you are out sick, watch your cat while you travel, or bring you Taco Bell when you forgot your lunch at home. Although having this kind of help is very useful, there is also an emotional need that is being met.

If you have a friend that you know would totally give you a ride somewhere if you needed it, you have an extra measure of security against being stranded somewhere. Similarly, it's nice to know that someone will have your back when things get tough.

Learning

Iron really does sharpen iron.

By definition, friendship is a connection between two distinct and diverse people. Just by being in proximity to the other, we learn ways of thinking and doing that are different than our own. Although learning may not be a survival need, it allows us to grow and surpass ourselves.

Sometimes, friends teach us practical skills. When Dan and I first became friends, he taught me how to do web development while I showed him how to lift weights. Fast forward a few years, and here I am giving a talk to the American Psychological Association about developing your online presence, and Dan just deadlifted 400 pounds.

Other times, friends teach us life lessons. We learn what it means to be compassionate, to share openly and freely, and to take risks. We learn how to work hard and discipline ourselves to reach new heights. And the best part is, you will never have too much learning. Each of us can continue to learn and be inspired indefinitely, always meeting new friends and discovering new ideas.

These five essential food groups of friendship do more than sustain us and help us survive - they enhance the human experience. Some of us may feel undernourished, starved even. But at least now you can begin to pinpoint which areas need to be fed.

Perhaps you have plenty of friends who are willing to give you rides or go places with you, but you lack the emotional support that empathy provides. Perhaps you find yourself spending too much time alone, wishing for a companion to come alongside you. Or, perhaps you feel stagnated in your friendships, no longer learning or growing with one another.

When people do not get enough of a particular nutrient, they can develop terrible health issues. If you starve yourself of protein, for example, your body will struggle to repair muscle tissues adequately, which results in feeling sore, tired, or even developing an injury. The same is true when it comes to relationships.

Consider the underfed areas of your friendship needs and how that might impact your day to day life. What is it like to try to survive without companionship, fun, or empathy? How does it feel when you need help around the house, but no one is there for you? Perhaps without knowing it, you have developed a few injuries along the way.

Just as relationships meet our needs in different ways, each of us is uniquely suited to help meet the needs of others. Everyone is gifted with particular talents and intuition that make it easier to notice and meet the needs of our friends. Some of you may be very good at providing practical assistance, while others may be better at empathy.

Take a moment to think about which of these needs you are best at meeting for others. Which ones come easily for you? Which ones do you struggle with?

Let's remember Dan's wisdom about the Jewish Proverb of the Spoons. The proverb says that heaven and hell are the same place: everyone is seated around a large bowl of soup while holding extremely long spoons. In hell, everyone tries to feed themselves, which is impossible to do with such utensils; meanwhile, in heaven, everyone uses their spoons to reach out and feed those sitting across from them. People in heaven are able to feed others and be fed in return, while those in hell starve for eternity.

You have the ability to meet the needs of others.

You might not have a super spoon, but you do have kind words, open ears, and helpful hands.

And that is what this book is all about.

Chapter Summary

Friendship helps meet our needs in so many different ways. I believe friendship meets five primary needs: Companionship, Fun, Empathy, Assistance, and Learning. As you discover what needs you lack the most, you will begin to understand what sorts of friends you are hoping to find.

Questions to Ponder:

- Who in your life seems to be best at meeting other people's needs?

- Do you ever feel drained, continually meeting the needs of others without genuinely feeling taken care of yourself?

CHAPTER 3
THE ANIMALS OF ATTACHMENT

Once upon a time, many years ago, you were born.

It's true!

More years for some and less for others, but few of us can recall those first few memories of precious life. This critical window of development has long been analyzed by psychologists and attachment theorists.

As a part of the vast animal kingdom, our species developed ways of working together to form relationships. Some say that we begin to learn to connect and love at our first breath, while others will say these lessons take time to sink in.

Regardless, each of us has learned how to form relationships and attach to others. And most of us have patterns of relating to one another.

When we form new relationships, including friendships, we tend to feel a certain way towards the other. Motivation, worry, attraction, disinterest. These feelings tend to crop up in other relationships, and over time we can see patterns of relating.

This chapter is all about helping you recognize and understand those patterns in your life.

Here is an example. When I make a new friend, I tend to try a bit too hard to make them like me. I tell funny stories to make them laugh, I bring them their favorite soda when we hang out, and I always worry if I am being a "good enough" friend. My friends will assure me that I am doing just fine and not to worry, but that doesn't always help, does it? Some of you might resonate with those feelings, and yet this might sound crazy or strange to others.

Dr. Mary Ainsworth wanted to understand why we act this way. Back in the 1970's, Dr. Ainsworth created a study called "The Strange Situation" where she would observe mother-child pairs in different situations to learn how the child was attached to their mother.

Here's what would happen in each scenario:

1. Mother and child would play with toys together in an observed room.

2. A stranger would enter the room and attempt to play with the child.

3. The mother would quietly leave the room.

4. The mother would return later to comfort the child.

Some of the children would shriek and cry when mother left, others would continue to play with their toys. These scenarios were designed to help us understand how we act in relationships, particularly when those relationships feel threatened.

Why would mother leave me in this strange situation?

How do I feel about this strange person looking down at me?

How should I act when mother returns?

Dr. Ainsworth grouped the way these children reacted, or attached, into three main groups. Since then, those groups have been broken down into categories called "attachment styles." I like to use cute little animals as metaphors to help people understand what those attachment styles mean. Each attachment style comes with specific needs about safety in relationships, and ways of responding when those relationships are threatened.

I call these *The Animals of Attachment*:

The Puppy

Puppies are pretty easy to get along with, right? They play happily when you are around, they become sad or worried when you leave, and they are ecstatic when you return. And, unless trained otherwise, puppies are good with strangers. Puppies are a great example of what secure attachment can look like. Most people who grow up in loving and stable homes with supportive family members and friends are able to develop secure attachment styles. When stressed, people with secure attachments are able to have their needs met by others as well as themselves. They tend to set healthy boundaries while also being open and authentic.

Relational needs:

- To feel safe, loved and understood
- Healthy attachment figures

Responses to threats:

- Seeks emotional support from their relationships
- Is able to cope with many difficult emotions on their own

The Cat

Cats tend to act differently than puppies. Cats will sometimes approach you and nuzzle your leg, as if they want to be held, only to squirm and claw at you as soon as you pick them up. They might run from you when you try to pet them, but then come to lay in your lap randomly while you watch television. Cats are a good example of what ambivalent (or mixed) attachment looks like. When stressed, people who are more ambivalent in their attachment may react in a variety of ways and can sometimes have difficulty having their needs met. People who are more ambivalent may have experienced a mixture of stability and instability during childhood, or perhaps they have dealt with loss or rejection.

Relational needs:

- To feel safe, loved and understood
- Sometimes will desire space or distance
- Sometimes will desire closeness from attachment figures

Responses to threats:

- May have difficulty expressing or having needs met
- May respond in a variety of ways, such as seeking support, lashing out, or becoming protective or guarded

The Tortoise

Tortoises are perfectly content munching on their lettuce and sitting in the shade. They do not seem to mind if we leave them alone, and they don't seem to want to play with others. Tortoises are tricky, though, because they may actually have needs for relationship and belonging that go unmet. Or, perhaps the tortoise has been hurt by others, and so it is safer to stay in the safety of their lonely shell than to reach out for connection. Tortoises show us what avoidant attachments may look like. People who are more avoidant of relationships tend to rely on self-soothing when they feel stressed, such as exercise or work, rather than reaching out to others. This is also fairly common among the autism community, although attachment and autism is an evolving area of research and perhaps less well understood than we might hope.

Relational needs:

- To feel safe, loved and understood
- Often will desire space or distance

Responses to threats:

- May have difficulty expressing or having needs met
- Will likely respond by withdrawing into their shell
- Relies heavily on self-soothing

The Hen

The hen spends her entire day watching her baby chicks and providing for them. Any time one chick wanders off, she rushes to bring it back to the nest. She devotes so much energy to others and constantly worries that her loved ones will leave her. When someone threatens her younglings, she springs into action and fights to the death to keep them safe. The hen illustrates what an "anxious" or protective attachment might look like. People who are more anxious in their relationships tend to be overly focused on what the other is thinking or feeling and attempt to meet their every need. They worry that others will leave them, and so they avoid taking risks or expressing their needs. People who are more like the hen tend to take care of others when they feel stressed, rather than take care of themselves.

Relational needs:

- To feel safe, loved and understood
- Safety and closeness with attachment figures

Responses to threats:

- May overexpress or overreact to have needs met
- Will likely respond in ways that protect the attachment figure
- Relies heavily on the wellbeing and approval of others to feel safe

These attachment styles help psychologists understand our relational habits, our default tendencies when we attach with others. These groups are not meant to capture every person's experience or personality, there are individual differences of course, but this is a good place to start. As you noticed, all of us desire safety in our relationships. Humans are herd animals by nature, which means each of us craves a space of belonging. And, we experience distress when we are rejected or isolated from the pack.

What attachment styles show us is that we all respond to relationships in different, but similar, ways. Our beliefs and actions in relationships are deeply rooted in how we attach, and so understanding our own attachment style can help us better respond to others.

Let's take a look at an example:

Louise and her new friend, Gene, decided to go to the park together to play. They went on the slides, they swung on the swings, and they raced each other across the jungle gym. During one of their races, a kid named Tina decides to join in. Louise notices that Tina and Gene seem to be having a lot of fun together, giggling and whispering to one another. Gene is so excited, "Look at all these new friends! I must be doing something right." Louise begins to feel worried – she thinks to herself, "What if Gene likes Tina more than me?" Her heart races and her cheeks burn with jealousy. Louise runs to Gene's side, grabs him by the wrist, and scoffs "We have to leave now, bye new kid!" as she marches Gene away from the park. Confused, Gene asks Louise what happened. Louise scowls at Gene, frustrated that he doesn't get it, and refuses to explain it to him. The next day, Gene doesn't really feel like spending time with Louise and turns down her next invitation.

Louise seems most like the cat or the hen in this example, right? A few of you might resonate with this story. Sometimes we feel worried that our friends will leave us for other people. Sometimes we feel like Gene, just trying to make new friends. And sometimes we feel more like Tina, confused and isolated, unable to interpret the strange social behaviors of others.

The funny thing is, each of us yearns for relationship. We are hardwired for belonging. Those feelings of worry and anger are there to help you preserve the friendship; after all, Louise did not want to lose her newfound friend Gene to some random kid on the playground! Yet, sometimes those same feelings can get in the way of maximizing our connections.

This is why we start our journey towards being a friend with attachment. Once you are able to understand your attachment style and how it informs your approach to relationships, you can unlock the secrets of friendship. You can avoid the pitfalls of insecurity and worry by being aware of your relational needs.

How to Avoid Attachment Pitfalls

Take a moment to think about your tendencies in relationships, or perhaps what attachment animal you most often embody. Do you feel more like the puppy, relatively secure and easy to get along with? Do you feel like the cat, with an odd mix of attachment and avoidance? Or do you feel like the tortoise, disconnected and riding solo? The answer to these questions may also vary from relationship to relationship. You may experience a more secure connection with your father while also having an ambivalent relationship with your friend or vice versa.

Here's a thought experiment that might help. Imagine for a moment that you and your best friend are playing video games together. Every few minutes, you notice your friend set down their controller to text someone on their cellphone. Do you feel tempted to pry and take a peek at who they are texting? You may be more like the hen and feel protective about the relationship. Do you ignore them and continue playing without care? You may be more like the puppy, feeling unthreatened by your friends' behavior. Do you feel angry and tell your friend you are tired, rather than authentically expressing yourself? You may be more like the tortoise, preferring to retreat and avoid confrontation. These feelings might be based on your attachment style, which in turn will guide your unique approach to relationships – and that is why your attachment style matters.

When you visit the ocean, you will see warnings about something called a riptide. Riptides are extremely powerful underwater currents caused by tidal flow. Swimmers can get caught in these riptides if they aren't careful, and the current will try to pull them farther out to sea. When you are caught in a riptide, you are not supposed to swim against it – you'll just exhaust yourself and drown. You also are not supposed to just lay back and float, because then the riptide will just continue pulling you farther from shore. Instead, you are supposed to swim across the current, parallel to the shoreline, until you escape.

Attachment pitfalls are similar to riptides. When we feel that our relationships are threatened, we easily fall back on our defaults, our relational habits. This is like letting the riptide take its course. Sometimes we try to fight against our attachment needs until we become exhausted and resigned. Rather than going with the flow, it might be time to try something new. Here are a few ideas to get you started:

1. **Notice when you feel threatened.** Pay attention when you begin to feel anxious, hurt, or angry in your relationships. Try to notice specific words or actions that trigger those feelings. You can begin to gather data about your attachment needs and how certain things may cause you to feel unwanted.

2. **Be curious and connect the dots.** Ask yourself why you feel that way. Reflect on what your emotional reaction makes you want to do – run away, cry, start an argument. What about the threat pulls that response from you? Try to connect the dots between what is happening and what has happened to you in previous relationships. Does the situation remind you of something from your past? Have you been hurt by similar words or actions before?

3. **Consider the consequences.** Think about the possible consequences of your instinctual reaction to the threat. If you decide to withdraw, you might avoid a conflict – but ultimately never get to express yourself. If you decide to start a fight, you might get to express yourself while also risking harm to the friendship. Ask yourself whether or not the outcome fits what you want in the relationship.

4. **Swim along the shore.** Rather than falling back on your default reaction, try something new. If you tend to withdraw, try opening up a bit. If you tend to be reactive or argumentative, try

to empathize with your friend before diving into conflict. You might also try sharing whatever feelings the other person's behavior evoked in you, such as "When you did [the thing], it made me feel [feelings]." Swimming along the shore can be challenging, and you will improve with practice.

No matter what attachment style you lean towards, you came to this book for a reason. Now you can see how your default patterns in relationships may emerge when you are trying to build new friendships. Keep these things in mind, we will talk more about attachment (and how to avoid pitfalls) later on.

Chapter Summary

Each of us learned how to relate and attach to others from a very early age. Over time, we developed habits or patterns known as "attachment styles" that guide how we act and feel in most relationships. I used animal metaphors to help simplify and explain these attachment styles and provided examples of what those might look like in the real world. Although our attachment needs are designed to help us maintain our relationships, sometimes our needs go unmet because of our behavior.

Questions to Ponder:

- What do you like and dislike about your attachment style?

- How has your attachment style affected your relationships?

- Where did your attachment style come from? Your parents? Your siblings?

CHAPTER 4
GUARDING YOUR CASTLE

I have always wanted to be a knight.

I think it started when I was around five years old. My grandmother gave me a book on medieval armor and knightly codes of honor, and I was hooked. I remember taping together cardboard boxes to make castles for myself. I was Sir Kyler the Brave, hero of the realm.

Although Sir Kyler was very knightly and gallant, he wasn't happy. His biggest problem was that he didn't enjoy spending time outside of his castle, which made it difficult to go on adventures, and there really was no room for people to visit and enjoy the crayon tapestries.

Medieval kings and queens would erect castles to house their kingdom and keep it safe from invasion. The grandest castles could withstand massive siege attacks with thick walls, deep moats, well-trained archers, and plenty of goods reserved to keep the kingdom fed. An incredible amount of resources would go into building the castle's defenses, and a well-defended castle felt safe for the royals.

The problem was, no matter how great the castle's defenses were, enemies could simply sit outside the gates and prevent supplies from entering or leaving. Rulers would become paranoid about spies entering the castle and create strict laws about who could and could not enter. Nearby kingdoms would notice these daunting defenses and respond by building more massive walls of their own. They would keep building and building, and in some cases, the castles became so heavy they would begin to sink into the ground.

Friendship is not medieval warfare. Not very often, anyway.

But, there is a lesson to be learned from castle defenses. Each of us has our own castle, a safe place where we house our innermost selves. We create interpersonal barriers and defenses to protect ourselves from stress, pain, and judgment.

Although our defenses can keep us safe from those things, they can also prevent good things like friendship from entering our lives. This chapter is all about helping you identify those barriers and discover how they might be getting in between you and friendship.

The Walls of Emotional Distance

Remember the story of when I said goodbye to my childhood friend? I think most of us would have felt wracked with sorrow at that moment; and yet, I do not remember feeling anything at all. No sadness, no worry. I was completely disconnected from my emotional experience.

Emotional distance, also known by psychologists as denial, is a defense mechanism that helps keep us from being overwhelmed with our emotional experience.

Here is an extreme example. Imagine you are driving down the road that passes along a massive river. A squirrel scurries across the street just ahead, and you swerve to miss it. Sadly, you lose control of the vehicle, careening into the icy cold river. You realize that you need to exit the car immediately, but your body is flooded with terror, hurt, and confusion. This would be a great moment for you to distance yourself from those feelings and focus on getting to safety.

Just like castle walls, this defense keeps certain threats from affecting us. Over time, our minds learn to prepare for future threats by building up the walls to withstand the stressors of life. These walls are very good at what they do. Too good, even.

We can lose touch with our emotional experience, and we become un-relatable to others. A potential friend may try to share how worried they are about an upcoming exam, but we aren't able to empathize or show compassion. This makes can make us come across as cold or uncaring. But this is not our fault.

Those of us who have experienced trauma may have the thickest walls of all. We have experienced the horrors of the human experience, and our minds will do whatever is necessary to keep that from happening again. This is particularly relevant when it comes to relational trauma, or painful experiences that occur between other people and us.

If you have ever felt betrayed by a loved one, for example, you may have a wall that keeps you from having that happen ever again. That wall may protect you by preventing you from connecting emotionally with other people, and thereby avoid having that connection abused in the future.

It's okay to have walls, especially because you might not have built them intentionally. Yet, your walls may be keeping you from receiving much-needed supplies of love and friendship.

The solution to managing these walls is difficult, but so worth it.

Here's a question: have you ever wondered how porcupines snuggle? Think about it. With all of those spiky quills, it makes you wonder why porcupines would even try. Nonetheless, porcupines have to get close at some point to survive – just ask my favorite researcher psychologist Dr. John Gottman, relationship expert and porcupine reproduction specialist.

Just like walls on a castle, porcupines have an arsenal of quills to help keep them safe from threats. And yet, they are able to navigate those defenses to get close to each other by being vulnerable with one another.

Vulnerability can be one of the most challenging friendship skills. This is particularly true for people who were raised in homes that discouraged emotional expression and open sharing.

Dr. Brene Brown, the queen of vulnerability, teaches that the key to vulnerability is courage. We must take the risk of being vulnerable and open, and that can be scary.

My suggestion: start small. Begin by opening up to people that feel safe and sharing feelings that feel less risky. Your brain wants to keep those walls up as long as it believes the threat is out there. By intentionally taking the courageous step of vulnerability, you will begin to feel safe again.

The Brambles of Bellyaching

Some castles developed unintentional, but effective, natural defenses to threats. For example, some castles became surrounded by masses of thorny plants called brambles. These kept enemies from easily approaching without being horribly poked and scratched, sometimes even trapped and unable to escape, and so most would avoid getting too close.

Sometimes, we feel miserable. Just downright crappy. They say that misery loves company, and I think that is very true. Although it can sometimes feel nice to vent and bellyache to other people, too much of that can deter even the most compassionate friends. People who are continually complaining about their stress and worry tend to come across as needy or difficult to manage.

Just like the castle brambles, hardship can crop up over time. We develop habits of communicating how overwhelmed we feel because we feel overwhelmed. Our primary means of coping then exists outside of ourselves, which makes us feel like we lack control and security. We become prickly and unpleasant to be around, and as others begin to distance themselves from us, our growing need for support goes unmet. Sometimes this is to help protect you from their own stress, and sometimes this is because your stress is too much for them to manage right now.

The key to avoiding this barrier to relationship involves a combination of self-care and balance in relationships.

First and foremost, we must take responsibility and ownership for being our own best friend. If you knew your best friend was not sleeping well, eating unhealthily, or overwhelmed at work, you would want to take action to help them, right?

The curious paradox is that we cannot seem to help ourselves as well as we help others. We want to be able to rely on our friends for support, but our friends should not always be our buffer to stress. The better care you take of your castle, the harder it is for nasty brambles to crop up. We'll learn more about self-care in the next chapter.

Next, even if we are masters of taking care of ourselves, it is helpful to communicate some of our needs to our friends so they can help and be good friends to us. Interpersonal psychotherapists talk about the importance of balancing how much we communicate our *alpha*, or positivity and goodness, and our *beta*, our difficulties and struggles.

Think about your interactions with past or current friends. Do some people tend to share more alpha, bragging about how awesome their lives are? Do others wallow in their stress and happily share their burden without considering your needs? Find the happy middle of alpha and beta, and you can avoid growing the brambles of bellyaching.

The Portcullis of Projection

The portcullis is the large, metal gate that drops down at the entrance of the castle. In medieval or fantasy films, this is what they open when the soldier at the top of the wall yells "Raise the gate!" This structure was used to determine what is let in and out of the castle. Often, people were sent away when they reached the portcullis. Perhaps the soldiers thought they were spies or saboteurs. The soldier's judgment would determine who and what was allowed to enter.

The same is true when it comes to relationships. Each of us constantly receives messages from other people, and not just on our cell phones. When those messages reach us, we make decisions about what we let in and what we send away.

The soldier at the gate has a job for a reason.

We do not want to just allow any and all messages to enter our thoughts and affect how we see ourselves. Otherwise, our sense of self would feel scattered, like an unstructured collage of other peoples' opinions of who we are without a solid sense of self. However, we also need to learn about and understand ourselves through others; otherwise our identity is entirely based on how we imagine ourselves to be. Your identity should be a work of art, built masterfully using information from yourself as well as for others.

When it comes to this defense, people tend to make one of two mistakes. Mistake number one, they leave their portcullis open and allow in all of the negativity and criticism sent their way. Over time, our kingdom becomes a place we no longer enjoy. We learn to stop loving ourselves. This is almost as unhealthy as mistake number two, where people keep their portcullis closed and ignore the advice others give to us.

We tend to avoid negative or uncomfortable messages. This is usually a good thing. We do not want to soak up all of the negativity that is sent our way. But sometimes we let some of those feelings in, and we add that to our identity collage. When people tell us we seem anxious or sad, those aren't necessarily descriptors for how we want to be seen. So, we react by denying those feelings or placing them on other people. I am not sad, you are. I am not overweight, that guy over there is overweight. By rejecting those messages and sending them somewhere else, also known as projection, we protect ourselves from feeling anxious.

Remember what Dr. Carl Rogers taught. If we are unable to honestly see and accept ourselves for who we are, change might be impossible. Sometimes other people want to help us and provide useful feedback. If we project helpful advice elsewhere, we lose opportunities to grow.

The Towers of Intellectualization

Castle towers were built to help us see far across the land and gain some perspective. This was an excellent defense strategy, as it allowed the castle military to have the advantage of anticipating enemy movements and noticing weaknesses in their strategy.

Many of us have towers of our own. We build them nice and tall, far above the castle itself to maximize our ability to see and understand the world. When threats approach, we notice them immediately and respond with the most refined interpersonal strategies.

And yet, the tallest towers tend to lose touch with the kingdom itself. We forget to think about how we feel, the down-to-earth stuff that lays close to the heart of our castle. From the peak of our tower, we are able to keep a safe distance from our feelings by thinking through our problems. This defense is known as intellectualization. Although there are some similarities to the defense of denial, as with the Walls of Emotional Distance, the Towers of Intellectualization are not designed to keep feelings at bay. Rather, they overanalyze and attempt to control every thought and feeling in the hopes of maintaining their goals.

People who rely heavily on the towers of intellectualization are often very good at problem-solving. They set their feelings aside in order to come up with the most rational way to reach their goals. Unfortunately, relationships do not tend to work that way. Love and friendship requires a certain level of emotional investment, and emotions are not always rational. If your tendency is to avoid your feelings by thinking them through, you may need to come down from your tower once in a while. Take the risk of making some irrational, feelings-based decisions. You never know what friendships you'll find down here.

Your castle is incredible. You have built up a distinctive structure of personality, likes and dislikes, quirks, and passions that make you unique in the realm. And you have also built up some defenses, many of which keep you safe from harm. Yet, some of these may also keep your friends and loved ones at bay.

Take some time to think about your interpersonal barriers. Why are they there? Perhaps something happened in your story, an interpersonal attack or difficult life event, which motivated your mind to protect itself from harm. Do you feel like your walls are so heavy that you have begun to sink? Are you overwhelmed and stressed to the point where others keep their distance to avoid being tangled up in your stuff? Have you allowed too much criticism to enter your life, or perhaps chosen to ignore some helpful insights from others? These are issues that may get in the way of you sharing your kingdom and connecting with others.

As you become more aware of your defenses, you will recognize ways that you can lower your guard, open up, and feel secure with yourself. Take good care of yourself, and be present. Keep track of how you feel around other people and how you respond to their messages. Let yourself experiment with being vulnerable in small ways to help create opportunities for connection.

Maintain a growth mindset and these things will get easier. I promise.

Chapter Summary

Each of us responds to life's challenges in unique ways. Over time, our minds learn how to cope by building up defenses to protect us from harm in the future. However, these defenses come with side-effects of disconnection and instability. We can learn to use our defenses appropriately and bring them down as needed. In turn, people will see us as more open, authentic, and secure. Your ability to be a good and enjoyable friend can increase as you work on these defenses and improve yourself every day.

Questions to Ponder:

- Do you have other defenses not listed in this chapter?

- Are there any particular memories associated with your defenses?

- What can you do to help lower your defenses and become more interpersonal?

CHAPTER 5
THE SECRETS OF SOCIAL FITNESS

Humans are one of the few creatures that struggle to fit in with their herd.

From humble nomadic beginnings, we realized that our chances of survival improve when we stick together. Time has proven the effectiveness of this strategy as nations rose and the family unit became the backbone of society. And yet, today we face a loneliness epidemic in spite of the incredible interconnectivity offered by today's technology.

Why is that?

Here is my guess. As we spend less time face-to-face and more time face-to-screen, we have begun to lose our social abilities. Many of us avoid speaking on the telephone with others and prefer the comfort and convenience of the text message. Rather than spending an evening sharing conversation with one another, we spend our evenings sharing a television show.

Don't get me wrong, technology is awesome. My love for technology is matched only by my love for nacho cheese. However, technology has begun to affect our relational functioning.

This is not the first time our inventions have changed the way we live. In days of old, to get from one floor of the shopping mall to the next, one would take the stairs. When your clothes needed washing, one might spend a good hour scrubbing them on a washboard with soap. Technologies like the escalator and the washing machine dramatically reduced the amount of physical activity we had to do each day. The unhappy consequence has resulted in issues with weight gain and sedentary behavior.

The solution? Fitness centers and workout programs. These provided us with autonomy in our physical fitness. Now, you get to choose when and how you burn your calories. We have to make the extra effort to be physically active.

I believe that the same is true when it comes to being social.

When you work out, you might choose to exercise specific muscle groups to help you meet your goal. The secret to social fitness is similar: find ways to use your less-used social muscles.

If becoming a good friend is your goal, there are four main muscle groups that you want to focus on: **Communication, Attunement, Remembrance,** and **Self-Regulation.** Let's dive in and learn how you can strengthen each of these areas.

Communication

Think of communication as the central core of all things social. Humans have quite the knack for communicating with one another. In fact, most evolutionary anthropologists agree that our propensity for communicating is responsible for the rapid advancement of our species.

And yet, we struggle! We struggle to share our thoughts of love and anger and joy with one another because we are, you guessed it, imperfect. But, the human brain is a beautiful machine, one designed to adapt and problem-solve and learn. Your mind can learn to communicate just as well as it can learn other things, like riding a bike or clipping your toenails.

So, how can we learn to communicate? If you go online looking for communication advice, you will find plenty of rich resources such as Dan's *Improve Your Social Skills* and *Level Up Your Social Life* designed to help you learn how to engage in small talk, maintain a conversation, and share with confidence.

I'll share a few pointers from Dan's books here, but I absolutely recommend diving into his material to learn more.

Good communication has three basic components: The message, the audience, and the response.

The Message

The message is whatever you are hoping to convey to the other person. Messages start with a thought or a feeling. We might have a friendship food group that is unmet, for example, which makes us feel lonely. Depending on our attachment style, these feelings motivate us to communicate in some way. The message might be simple, such as a first-time introduction. "Hi, my name is Kyler." Or the message might be more complex, such as a first "I love you" or "I think we could be great friends." Sometimes the message involves words, but we as humans also rely heavily on nonverbal means of communicating.

Learning to be a good message sender takes time and practice, but here are a few tips to help get you started:

1. **Let yourself mess up.** People tend to silently sit and frantically piece together the perfect way to articulate their message, and by the time you are ready the conversation has moved on without you. We do this because we are afraid of how we might come across. It feels better to keep our mouths shut and be seen as the quiet one than to open our mouths and become the loud foolish one. The problem is, even the loudest and most foolish people are able to get their message across. It is okay to fumble your words and say stupid things, you will get better. And your friends will still love you.

2. **If you aren't sure what to say, try to start off a sentence with "I feel like…".** For example, "I feel like I should say something, but I can't think of anything to say." Or, "I feel like you and I are becoming closer as friends." This is a trick that psychologists will use in therapy when they are trying to identify emotions or simply further the conversation. This is also a great way to show your audience that you were listening to their message, which encourages them to continue the conversation with you.

3. **Get feedback.** Sometimes it can be difficult to ask for help, particularly when it comes to social skills. But here's the secret: most people love giving other people advice. After you get done with a conversation, try asking your audience how you did. Sometimes you can even tell them that you are working on improving your conversation skills, if that helps. Although you might get some critical feedback that feels unpleasant, you will also start to hear about the things you are doing well. Sometimes it can also be helpful to get professional help, in which case you can hire a social skills coach or a therapist to help you master the art of messaging.

The Audience

Your audience awaits! The audience plays an important role in your communication because, well, otherwise you are just talking to yourself. Which is fine, as long as you aren't talking back. When it comes to having your message received, there are two important things to ask yourself when it comes to your audience:

1. **Are they paying attention?** Not everyone is good at paying attention to one another, and sometimes we get distracted by things that pull us out of our conversation. The easiest way to tell if your audience is paying attention is to use what Dan calls "Red Light" and "Green Light" body language. These are used to describe the audience's posture, facial expression, and eye contact. Just like at a traffic light, we watch for the right signal to indicate if we stop or go. Green Light body language tends to include an open and relaxed posture, facing towards you with their feet and/or shoulders, and good eye contact. Red Light body language signals us to stop sending messages for now, the other person has lost interest or attention. We can tell someone is giving us Red Light body language if they are not facing towards us, if they appear tense or uncomfortable, and if they are looking away or seem disengaged. People will give the Red Light for a variety of reasons, and it isn't necessarily because of something you said or did. Although it can be hurtful to notice

someone giving us the Red Light, it is important to recognize how that might affect the message being received.

2. **Is your message a good fit?** In other words, is your message appropriate for the context? For example, you might really want to share your thoughts about *Mad Max: Fury Road* but doing so during a funeral service is probably not the best fit. Similarly, you might not want to talk about the violence in *Mad Max* if your audience is only four years old. These are extreme examples, of course. A more practical example would be trying to share something with someone who is in a hurry. You may have a well-articulated message and they might be paying attention, but your message might be making them late for a meeting. If the message is "the meeting is canceled," then that is a good fit. If the message is, "Did you watch the last episode of *The Bachelor*?" it probably isn't. Unless, of course, they announced that the meeting is canceled during that episode, in which case it is, but that seems less than likely.

The Response

So, you have articulated your message, your message is appropriate, and the audience paid attention.

Your work is not done, my friend.

Now comes perhaps the most important piece of communication: receiving and interpreting the response. The response is whatever reaction your audience has from your message. They might respond with a verbal message of their own, or they might message you non-verbally with a facial expression, a change in posture, or even just a nod. This response is such a crucial element, and too many of us tend to miss it. Here are a few things to keep in mind when interpreting the response:

1. **Does their response make sense?** For example, if you just made a really killer poop joke to an appropriate audience, we would hope that they might laugh or at least smile. But if they suddenly frown or become tense, the message may not have been appropriate. Unless, of course, you intended to anger or gross

out your audience. Which I have to say, that's really not the best strategy for making new friends. A good rule of thumb is to try to anticipate how the audience will react to your message, and then see how it matches after you send it. If the reaction is equal to the intent, then well done! If not, you can always apologize and make repairs (more on this in Part 3).

2. **Are you messaging as much and as often as they are?** Sometimes we really want to share something, but we don't always give our audience space to respond (or vice versa). The key to making sure your communication partner remains engaged in the conversation, and therefore will be receptive to additional messages, is to try to match the other person's amount and frequency of sharing. If you find yourself rattling away to the point where the other person could go make a sandwich and eat it before you get done talking, you are sharing too much. If your partner seems to be trying to maintain the conversation by themselves, and you are having trouble knowing what to say, you are probably not sharing enough. Balance the sharing between you and your audience can take time to master. Sometimes it helps to get feedback from your partner, which can be as simple as asking "am I saying too much," or having someone casually observe you in conversation.

3. **Were you paying attention?** It's easy for us to get wrapped up in our own message to the point where we are not paying sufficient attention to the audience. Once your message is sent, you become the audience. You and the other will swap roles until the encounter is finished. Pay close attention to the messages others send your way, so that when they finish sharing you are ready to react and respond appropriately. A simple hack that psychologists use is the "It sounds like…" sentence, where you try to summarize the other person's message in a short one-liner. For example, if my friend has just finished telling me about their weekend I might say "It sounds like you had a lot of fun! What was your favorite part?"

Keep in mind the messages you send, read your audience, and observe how your messages evoke responses in others. As you master the skill of communication, you will be amazed at how much more present and engaged you feel in your relationships.

Attunement

If you could pick one superpower, what would it be?

Some might say super strength. Others might say the ability to fly. And some might say they wish they could read peoples' minds.

Well, ladies and gentlemen and everyone in between, that last one is possible. Although we cannot hope to perfectly read thoughts, we are able to empathize and understand what someone else might be experiencing.

The ability to understand and empathize with others is central to becoming a good friend. Even if you are terrible at communicating, the capacity to attune to the emotional experience of others allows you to anticipate needs and be there in ways that other people are not.

You have probably experienced attunement in your everyday life without realizing it.

Here is an easy example. Think of the last time you watched a spooky movie. During the film, you may have noticed your heart begin to race or your thoughts begin to feel somewhat frantic during particularly frightening scenes. We experience these feelings because we have entered into the world of the characters on the screen. Our minds are capable of what psychologist Dr. D.J. Siegal calls *mindsight*, or the capacity to embody someone else's thoughts and feelings at any given moment. We feel afraid during scary movies because we can imagine what the character might be feeling, which then recreates their experience in us.

This is the secret to attuning to our friends or potential friends. You can imagine what the other person is thinking or feeling simply by being open to imagining their lived experience. If I were to ask you to imagine how Harry Potter felt while dueling Voldemort, you could probably drum up a sense of what that was like for him. Is he happy and excited for the big fight? Probably not. Is he nauseous and queasy? Maybe a little. Is he scared, angry, and determined? Most likely.

The skill of attunement can be learned with practice. Psychologists are trained to do this without even thinking. In therapy we sit with people and learn to attune to experiences of sadness, grief, worry, excitement, and rage. And you can do these things, too.

Attunement has three basic components: *awareness, identification of emotion,* and *openness.*

Awareness

The first step to attuning to someone else's emotional experience requires a certain level of awareness. You must be watching and listening for cues that indicate what the other person is experiencing at the moment.

This level of awareness is not easy to do, at first. After all, this is a big part of what therapists get paid to do. You must maintain a stance of curiosity and observation regarding the other person. Imagine yourself as an emotional data collector, taking mental notes in an attempt to understand the phenomena of someone else's mind.

Identification of Emotion

As you maintain an awareness of the other person's experience, you will begin to piece together indicators of their emotional process. Perhaps they have told you about a fight they had with a loved one which ended with hurtful words being exchanged. Perhaps they just found out they were awarded a raise at work. Or, perhaps they have been looking down at their feet, a solemn look on their face, while they wring their hands nervously. All of these things are data that you can use to identify their emotional experience.

Some of us, myself included, struggle to put some feelings to words. And that is okay, we will get better at it together. But for now, you can rely on the basics: happy, sad, angry, disgusted, and bored. If you can learn to identify those five emotions, you have yourself a starter pack for identifying more complex emotions, like hangry or puzzled.

Openness

Finally, in order to be fully attuned to your friend's experience, you must be open and willing to experience some of what they are feeling. Allow yourself to explore some of that sadness or that joy. Embrace the beauty that is the human emotional experience.

Remember, your emotions are a sensory organ. If your friend offered you a cupcake and said "wow, this is super chocolatey!" you would probably allow yourself to taste that chocolate goodness, rather than deny yourself that experience of attunement.

Sometimes our friends are experiencing uncomfortable emotions, such as worry or sadness. Your attunement to those emotions can help lift their spirits and help them feel understood. This is why attunement is such an essential friendship skill.

You can learn to attune to the emotional worlds of other people. If you remember to listen and be aware, notice signs of emotional experience, and allow yourself to be open to sharing those experiences, you will unlock the secret of attunement.

Remembrance

Do you remember? The 21st night of September?

Memory is perhaps the most underrated area of friendship fitness. In fact, very few relationship help books touch on the importance of memory.

Perhaps they forgot.

Remembrance is a word used to describe the action of accessing memory. Our brains are very good at storing all sorts of data, often without even trying. However, when it comes time to remember stored data, such as during that exam you forgot to study for, your brain struggles with the retrieval process.

Your ability to remember things about your friends can have a significant impact on those relationships. Think about how you feel when a friend sends you a gift on your birthday or shows up at your piano recital. Think about how you feel when they forget. Or at least, when it seems like they forgot. Your friend may very well have remembered those things, but unless they did something with those memories you would never know.

Yet, this isn't just about remembering certain dates or events. You also want to remember what I call "friend facts." What is your friend's favorite food? What music do they like? Where did they grow up?

These tidbits of information help send messages about you as a friend. One, it lets them know that you are paying attention to what they say. Our friends love to feel seen and heard, and when you remember how they offhandedly mentioned their passion for Etherwood or The Lumineers it makes them feel good. And two, it shows that you are curious about them and invested in their story. This sends the message that you are dedicated to the friendship and that you enjoy their company.

Learning how to be better about remembrance can take time, but I believe in you. You might be better at it than you think. Here are a few hacks that you can use to get started.

Remembrance Hack #1: Ask Good Questions

Ask friends and potential-friends questions about themselves. By asking good questions, you can begin to add data to your friendship fact storage. You have to know things to remember them.

Asking questions can be tricky, though, as there is a fine line between curious and creepy. Creepy questions can be avoided with one simple trick.

Imagine for a moment that we were going to sit down and write everything there is to know about you onto notecards. Next, we would sort those notecards into ten separate boxes. After we line up the boxes side by side, we would put the least sensitive stuff, like your favorite foods or where you went to high school, in the first box. We would then put all of the most sensitive stuff, like your deepest darkest secret or whether you are Team Edward or Team Jacob, in box number ten. The rest of your information would be sorted into the other boxes depending on how sensitive it is, with the most sensitive going towards the tenth box and the least towards the first.

Now, imagine how you would feel if a stranger came up and started asking for stuff out of box number ten. That feels pretty scary, right? If they asked for stuff out of box number one, you would probably be more okay with that.

Early in your friendship, start with questions that feel safe and could easily fit in box number one. What is your favorite food? Do you like bowling? Are you a cat person or a dog person? As your friendship deepens and you develop trust with one another, you begin to trust people with stuff from boxes two through ten. The same is true for your friends.

Remembrance Hack #2: Write Stuff Down

If you struggle with remembering things like birthdays or plans to meet up with someone, try writing it down.

Now, you do not want to carry around a sinister looking moleskin notebook that says "Everything I Know about My Beloved Friends" on the cover. Don't do that.

Instead, you might try putting notes in your phone or adding calendar reminders for important dates. You might also try keeping a personal journal where you can write about your day and keep track of things your friends tell you. Writing improves the brain's chances of retaining information, which means that you will be more likely to remember it even if you wrote it down and threw it away.

Remembrance Hack #3: Apologize and Make Up

No matter how good your memory is or how detailed your notes are, you are going to forget things about your friend. You might order their least favorite pizza or forget to show up to their basketball tournament.

Rather than denying or ignoring the fact that you forgot, you can show your friend that you care more about them than being right by saying sorry. You are human, and being human means you will make mistakes. Find ways to make it up to your friend and try harder to remember in the future.

On the flip side, your friends will forget things about you. Extend your friends the same grace you would want for yourself. The best friends continue to forgive and forget because they are committed to the relationship.

You can give your friends the incredible gift of feeling understood and important. As you learn about others and demonstrate your attentiveness and curiosity through remembrance, people will notice.

Self-Regulation

Several years ago, I went to this huge birthday party for one of my friends.

The evening kicked off to a great start. There was cake, music, and lots of people to meet and spend time with. People were laughing and having a good time, and my friend seemed to be having a great birthday.

About an hour in, someone made an insensitive comment about the LGBTQ+ community. People pushed back, the commenter apologized, and the matter seemed settled for the most part as the celebrations continued. However, one partygoer (we'll call him Grover) became particularly upset. Grover became tearful and angry, and he screamed at the commenter. He then stomped off to lock himself in the bathroom. You could cut the tension in the room with a knife. The joyous mood of the party was snuffed out, and several people decided to leave. My friend's birthday came to a screeching halt.

Grover later emerged from the bathroom, embarrassed and apologetic. My friend was furious with the person that started it all, and so was I. But I can't help but feel like the party could have continued if Grover was able to manage his reaction to the situation. If Grover was able to regulate his emotions, allow himself to feel safe and unthreatened, and focus on enjoying the experience of the party, the night might have continued as planned.

Things like this happen all the time in our relationships. Everyone makes mistakes. We say things that inadvertently offend and cause hurt feelings. We overreact and retaliate with anger and sadness. Little misunderstandings turn into raging interpersonal battles, and no one walks away unscathed.

The best friends are able to manage their reactions and maintain composure. Psychologists refer to this as self-regulation, or the ability to control emotional reactions. Self-regulation takes time and practice to master, especially for people who have survived abuse or other traumatic events. However, just like the other areas of friendship fitness, self-regulation is a muscle that can be strengthened.

When we are hurt and angered by the things that happen to us, those emotions happen for a reason. Your body is designed to respond to threats through the **fight, flight**, or **freeze** response. Sometimes, we become aggressive and try to lash back and defend ourselves. Sometimes, we become fearful and try to escape. And sometimes, we lock up and become speechless. Each of these threat responses has deep evolutionary roots that help keep you alive and healthy. If a bear charges towards you, your body will do whatever it takes to survive.

However, these survival reactions sometimes activate when there is no real threat. For example, during my friend's party, someone made an offensive comment. Although the comment may be interpreted as rude or hateful, the words themselves were not life-threatening. If the comment was aggressive or threatening in nature, then an equally forceful response may have been in order.

But most of the time, our friends do not make threats. More often than not, a misunderstanding or miscommunication sparks a small flame of conflict which we catalyze with our emotional responses.

Self-regulation happens in three phases. First, we must be aware of our current emotional state. Second, we must determine if our emotional state is appropriate for the situation. And third, we cope with our emotions to help redirect internal processes into something useful.

Phase One: Awareness

Your emotions are the sixth sense you never knew you had.

When you taste the sweet nectar of a Diet Mountain Dew, your brain combines the perceptions of sweet, citrus, and tangy to produce a distinct sensation. You do the same thing when it comes to your emotions. Your brain combines sensory information, along with previous memories and schemas, to produce emotional responses to help you interpret the situation.

Everyone has distinct emotional responses to their environment. These experiences depend on a vast number of variables, such as your life history, neurological physiology, and how you were raised. Autistic people have particularly unique configurations for how this process works. They can experience deep emotional sensations from particular stimuli that most neurotypical folks do not. Just as each of us has preferences for different kinds of foods and styles of clothing, we each come equipped with special ways of processing emotions.

As you become more aware of your unique emotional process, you will get better at identifying the things that kick off your fight-flight-freeze response. Psychologists call these "triggers," or things that are particularly good at inducing emotional reactions. Not all triggers are bad, however. For example, if I asked you to think of movie theater popcorn, that might trigger some happy memories.

Practice checking in with yourself and your emotional experience on a regular basis, especially when you are around other people. Sometimes you can start off by noticing what emotions you feel while watching television or reading a book, as you experience feelings of anger or fear during certain scenes. Pay attention to the things that evoke the strongest emotions, and try to identify what elements are particularly triggering.

Your awareness can act as a preemptive strike for triggering events. If you know that comments about your hair will set you off, you are able to recognize your response before it happens.

Phase Two: Evaluation

Imagine you went to McDonald's and ordered yourself a hamburger without onions, but your burger comes to you donned in nasty onion grossness. How would most people react?

Would they scream and throw the burger at the nice lady running the cash register? Probably not, although a quick search on YouTube tells us that this does happen from time to time. Although McDonald's rage videos are entertaining to watch, you never want to see yourself on one.

You want your emotions to serve you, rather than vice versa. Your feelings play an important role in motivation and communication, and so of course you should allow yourself to feel upset when something wrong happens to you. However, you should consider how much emotion is actually needed to accomplish your goal.

Phase Three: Redirection

The most challenging step in self-regulation happens here, where you actually do the regulating bit.

Now that you are aware of your emotional experience, you can evaluate whether or not your internal reaction is normal based on the situation. This is easier said than done, especially when you are in the heat of the moment, but practice makes perfect.

When the situation sparks too much emotion than is necessary, I suggest that you respond in the same way you would if you were on fire: **stop, drop**, and **roll**.

Stop. Pause for a moment. You may not need to respond immediately, so give yourself a moment to breathe and think. Allow yourself some space to reflect on the feelings you are experiencing, and consider the possibilities of the moment. Think about what matters most.

Drop. Try to lower your emotional state just a bit. Sometimes it can be helpful to try to tell yourself D-T-I-P, or Don't Take It Personally. People may say or do things to us that are unintentionally hurtful, and when we blow up in their faces things tend to escalate. Tense the larger muscles in your body, such as your legs and core, for a few moments and then rest. Notice as your heart rate and your breathing become within your control.

Roll. Roll has two meanings. You may have been able to drop your emotional state and simply roll with it, allowing yourself to stay engaged with the situation. If not, you may need to roll, or exit the situation for the moment. If you need to roll, as in leave, do your best to maintain good social etiquette and preserve the relationship. Sometimes you can ask to continue the conversation later or to change the subject. When this happens, it may also be important that you circle back to them to explain happened.

Our friends and loved ones sometimes make mistakes or say stupid things, for such is human. As you learn to stop, drop, and roll you, will notice that you are better able to redirect your emotional process and continue to engage in important relationships.

Bonus: The Doormat's Dilemma

Self-regulation is key for avoiding emotional blow-ups and unnecessary conflict; however, sometimes we need to stick up for ourselves. Many of us are guilty of letting people walk all over us, like a doormat. As someone who admittedly takes on the role of doormat more often than I would like, I should know.

We want to be sociable and friendly in our relationships. Sometimes this means we will bite our tongue or turn the other cheek when others say dumb or hurtful things. When we let those things slide, even when they are excruciatingly painful, we begin to neglect ourselves.

Remember to voice your needs in those moments of hurt. If someone makes an insensitive comment about your identity, your beliefs, or even your appearance, those are words you do not have to tolerate. However, using self-regulation skills can help you to communicate your hurt in a way that will be heard to others. Rather than flipping over the table or throwing a baked potato at someone's face, you can become aware of the situation, make an evaluation, and redirect your emotions in a way that helps you be the bigger person.

Putting it All Together: Your Social Fitness Plan

Personal fitness trainers are really good at doing two things: one, designing workout programs that help you meet your goals, and two, providing you with motivation and inspiration to keep moving forward. In order to meet your social goals, you will want to do the same.

Your personal plan may be different depending on your needs, but here are a few ideas to get you started. First, set your goal. Choose one area of social fitness you want to work on first. Next, set objectives that you can try to meet every day, every week, and every month. Your daily objective should be simple and easy. You might choose to work on remembering the names of people you meet, or perhaps you can work on attuning to the emotions of one person each day. Your weekly objective should be a bit more challenging, and your monthly objective should be something that pushes your social limits. Here's an example:

Social Fitness Plan

Goal: Improve my communication skills

Daily Objective: Say "Hello" and smile at one stranger every day.

Weekly Objective: Start a conversation with someone that lasts at least five minutes.

Monthly Objective: Go to one major social event and do not just hang out by the chips and dip.

Sometimes it can be difficult to work on new goals or stick to certain lifestyle changes. Fear not, you will learn how to make these changes stick in Chapter 7. In the meantime, begin to craft a social fitness plan that feels good and will help move you closer to your goals.

Chapter Summary

Learning to improve your social skills takes time and effort. Focus on learning how to communicate, attune to others, remember friendship facts, and regulate your emotions. As you become more sociable and comfortable around others, you will begin to reap the rewards of friendship and deeper connection.

Questions to Ponder:

- What social skills do you feel you are best at using?

- Have you noticed any social skills that need improvement? How do you want to work on those?

- What helps you feel more confident when using your social skills? Are there ways you can lean on this to help you grow in areas you feel less confident?

CHAPTER 6
PUTTING ON YOUR OXYGEN MASK

A good friend is a healthy friend. We want to keep ourselves emotionally, psychologically, and physically healthy enough to be able to enjoy and engage in friendship fully. We also live as mortal beings in an unpredictable chaotic world, which means that sometimes our health is compromised.

Although we cannot always prevent disease and dysfunction from taking space in our lives, each of us has the power to minimize risk.

Remember the Brambles of Bellyaching? When we are overwhelmed with stress and sickness, it is very difficult to be a good friend. It is also very difficult to be a good friend to someone who treats themselves poorly.

Yes, friendship can help meet our needs and support us when things are tough, but we want our relationships to be reciprocal and balanced. The best way to do this is to actively work on your own health and wellbeing.

Think of it this way. Every time you get on an airplane, the flight attendants give some very helpful instructions. They tell you that in the event of loss of cabin pressure, oxygen masks will descend like spaghetti monsters above each passenger. Your responsibility is to put your own mask on *first* before helping others. Why? Once you have your own mask securely fastened, you are less likely to pass out and more likely to be able to help others.

This chapter is all about helping you put your mask on first.

We couldn't hope to capture all of the facets of healthy living in one book, let alone one chapter, and so I will cover the top four: *Physical, Psychological, Social,* and *Spiritual.* Let's take a look at each of these to help identify what areas of your life may need an extra boost to get you back on track.

Physical: Tending to Your Garden

Everyone has a unique and complex physical form. They say your body is a temple, but I think that's a dumb metaphor. Once built, temples stop growing. Temples also don't need much maintenance to retain structure and do their job.

So, I think your body is more like a garden. A wonderful, complex garden that requires nurturing and hard work to keep it healthy. I grew up on a farm and helped raise plenty of gardens in my time, and so I like to think of myself as a bit of an expert. But really, my mom taught me everything there is to know when it comes to real life *Stardew Valley*. Thanks, momma!

There are three basic rules for keeping a garden healthy: keep it watered, keep it weeded, and make sure it gets the right amount of sunlight.

Keeping it Watered

I love food. So. Much. If I had to choose between air and food, I would probably happily suffocate while mowing down a sleeve of Oreos.

I imagine you also love food. Food is good.

Although plants don't necessarily eat water, the water definitely helps them grow and rejuvenate their cells. You have to water plants just the right amount to help them grow and produce fruits and vegetables. Too much water and the roots can rot or grow too shallow, which means a good windstorm will certainly knock the plant down or break it. Not enough water and the plant will wither and burn up in the sunlight, or focus its energy on staying alive rather than producing.

Similarly, your body needs the right amount of food (and water) to stay healthy.

Let me first say that I am not a nutritionist or a physician. However, in my day job I am constantly working with folks who have unbalanced intake behaviors. Too much food and drink, or too little, can lead to a host of medical issues: diabetes, blood pressure issues, heart failure, difficulty with focus and attention, back and joint pain, stroke, and much more.

How do you know how much food is the right amount? Here are a few things to look for:

1. **How is your energy level?** It's counterintuitive, but too much food can lead to lower energy levels. Similarly, if you aren't eating enough your body may feel weak or unmotivated. A good rule of thumb is to start with *My Fitness Pal* to look at how many calories you eat per day. If you are eating above or below the recommended amount for your age and activity level, you may want to make some changes to see how that affects your energy. Additionally, some people do not get enough vitamins with their daily intake. If you aren't currently taking any vitamins, consider consulting with your doctor or a nutritionist to see what might be useful to incorporate.

2. **Are you pooping?** Ah yes, the poop question. The frequency of your bathroom trips might help answer the question of how much food you should be having. The time constraints work can affect how often we have the chance to use the toilet, so sometimes it helps to start by looking at your days off. Most doctors (including Dr. Alana Biggers on *Healthline*) report that people poop about once per day, with a great deal of variation based on activity level, age, and amount of food eaten. Healthier people tend to poop around twice per day, less healthy folks will poop as little as once every three days. The poop question isn't just about how much you are eating, however; it's about the activity level of your gastrointestinal tract. Being active for at least 15-30 minutes per day can help keep your GI tract active, which means more poops and more smiles. Talk to your primary care provider if you have further poop questions, those are their favorites.

3. **Do you eat enough plants?** First of all, let me say that although grains and corn are technically plants, tortilla chips do not count as a salad. I am talking about plants that are freshly harvested and unprocessed, such as raw apples, carrots, lettuce, and peppers. A good rule of thumb is to imagine if the chosen plant could have been on the vine or tree only moments before you ate it. If it had to be pickled or fried first, it doesn't count. I am a big fan of adding more to your diet, rather than cutting things out. Instead of saying "no more cake," I tell people to eat an extra bowl of carrots before they eat their cake.

Of course, keeping your garden adequately watered requires much more than we can cover here. But this is a book on friendship, not dieting. If you can keep your garden healthy enough for people to visit and enjoy the fruits of your friendship, you are doing something right.

Keeping it Weeded

Weeding a garden can be a real pain. You spend hours stooped over, plucking nasty spikey weeds from the earth while the sun screams at your sweaty backside.

Weeding is also very important. No matter how healthy you might try to keep the garden, weeds can undo all of your hard work. They creep up slowly, choking out nutrients and hogging all the sunlight.

Life is full of weeds, or habits that invade our healthy bodies and take up valuable resources. Think about the weeds that might get in your way of having a healthy body. For some, this might be reliance on drugs such as nicotine, marijuana, or alcohol. For others, this might be reliance on unhealthy behaviors, such as self-harm or gambling. These weeds cost time, money, and energy that we can't afford to lose. Plus, most weeds directly affect health by causing serious issues like liver disease and cancer.

Just like weeding a garden, pulling out lifestyle weeds can be a real pain.

If your weeds are holding you back from having relationships and being healthy, it doesn't have to be this way. You have the power to change. But you don't have to do it alone. Sometimes we can do it on our own, but the easiest way to weed a garden quickly is to get help. Help might be a therapist, but it can also be a friend or a mentor who gives you the support you need.

The Right Amount of Sunlight

Here's a fun fact. Did you know that plants convert sunlight into nutrients through photosynthesis? Of course you do, you smart and handsome devil. However, a good balance of sunlight is needed to help the plant grow.

Think of sunlight as stimulation. Your body needs stimulation to stay active and healthy, just like the rays of the sun help stimulate the process of growth in plants. More specifically, your body needs to be active enough to know that it isn't dying. I have heard many physicians tell their patients that the day they stop walking is the day the body starts to die. As morbid as that might be, there is truth to that warning.

Your body is incredibly good at adapting to its environment. If your body knows that it needs to be prepared to sit all day on the couch playing *Overwatch*, then it will adapt by giving you plenty of padding and long-term storage. Although playing video games can be a great way to stimulate your brain, the rest of your body needs just as much stimulation. If your body knows it needs to be able to lift heavy weight and run a mile without stopping, it will build up muscle mass and lung capacity to help you survive. You don't want to be spending all of your waking hours in the gym, though. You want to be out in the world, making friends, earning money, and eating pizza.

So, how do you get the right amount of physical stimulation? Here are a few ideas to get you started.

1. **Start with baby steps**. People tend to be motivated and enthusiastic when they first start a new workout program, and they often end up overdoing it. Even if you have been active in the past, you should always start easy and work up to a higher

level of difficulty over a period of weeks and months. It is okay to start with something as simple as walking or standing for five to ten minutes at a time. You will get stronger, and your body will thank you for it. Plus, no matter how slow you go you are lapping everyone who spends their day holding down the couch cushions.

2. **Find the zone of optimal challenge.** As you become fit and the workouts get easier, it is time to turn up the heat a bit. This is another area where people make mistakes. Either they keep their workout the same and stop improving, or they ratchet up the difficulty too much. You want to get yourself somewhere in between too easy and too difficult, the zone of optimal challenge. The zone should keep you sweating and your heart rate up without making you feel like you are going to collapse.

3. **Be consistent.** Inconsistency is the kiss of death when it comes to fitness. Over time we lose progress, skip workouts, and eventually stop being active altogether. Even if you commit yourself to one workout per week, and you stick to it religiously, that sort of consistency will benefit you in the long run. The secret to consistency is accountability. Do whatever it takes to keep yourself on track – set reminders or alarms on your phone, put motivational sticky notes across from your toilet, tell a friend to ask you about your workouts every once in a while.

Your garden might have weeds. Some of the plants might be withered or unkempt. You might have forgotten to water it.

And that's okay.

Now you have a plan, and you are ready to nurture and care for your garden with renewed passion and awareness.

You can do this.

Psychological: The Master Bladesmith

The reason I kick off this chapter on self-care with physical and psychological health is because the mind and body are inseparably intertwined. Taking care of your body is essential for taking care of your mind, and vice versa. Illnesses such as depression and anxiety create significant physical issues, such as high blood pressure and digestive issues, while diabetes and drug abuse can also create significant psychological issues, such as psychosis and addiction.

Yet, psychological issues tend to be difficult to manage when our bodies are unhealthy. Now that you have a sense of how to keep your garden growing, you are ready to dive into the art of psychological health.

Think of your mind as a sort of blade, and you are the bladesmith. Swords were the popular choice of armament among ancient warriors, but you can imagine your mind to be whatever blade you want. Every blade is uniquely suited to fulfill some sort of purpose. Even the cheese knife has the noble quest of slicing processed dairy goodness for my sandwich. However, each blade must be cared for to keep its shape and sharpness.

As the master bladesmith of your own mind, you are tasked with three things: repair, maintenance, and improvement.

Repairing Your Blade

Sometimes, our blades get chipped. We face incredible challenges and hardship in our lives, and even when we work through them we suffer wear and tear.

Even the greatest knights broke their swords in combat.

Repairing a broken blade takes time and effort. Sometimes we try to ignore our own brokenness and charge into battle anyways. And yet, we aren't as effective. We struggle at work and in our relationships because our thoughts and feelings get in the way. It can be incredibly frustrating to notice the areas of our lives that used to be functional, but no longer work the way we want.

The good news is, no matter how shattered you might feel, your blade can be repaired.

Step up to your forge. Time to go to work.

It's not always easy, but it is possible. If you ever feel overwhelmed with repairs, it always helps to call in a specialist. Therapists help people through the brokenness every day. They spend years studying the science of psychology for just this purpose.

Let me equip you with some of their wisdom:

1. **Recognize the brokenness.** The first and most important step is to recognize that your blade might have chips or cracks in some places. Think about the difficulties in your life and how those have impacted your ability to think positively, concentrate, or learn and grow. These are the normal wear and tear of the human experience. You might also notice larger breaks or bends that represent the warfare of traumatic life events and loss. These too are part of life, and they can be repaired.

2. **Put the pieces back together.** When we experience the clash of stress and difficult life events, sometimes we lose pieces of who we are. In our anger and sadness, we might leave those pieces on the battlefield. We lose the capacity for love or forgiveness. We lose humor, creativity, and playfulness. But, these pieces are not forsaken casualties of warfare. Like the shards of Narsil, we can re-forge and rebuild the parts of ourselves we thought were long lost.

3. **Mend with time and self-compassion.** You are not fully responsible for any of your brokenness. Since the dawn of upright-walking humans, our species has harmed and broken one another through violence and abuse. Generations of revenge and rage and despair have passed these feelings on to us, and so we bear the burden of ancient sins. Each of us is broken in some way. We come from broken stock and live in a broken world. And that is okay. Things will get better. Give yourself space to reintegrate the broken pieces. Allow yourself some self-compassion and speak to yourself the way a kind friend might.

Maintaining Your Blade

In *Game of Thrones*, Tyrion Lannister says that books are like a whetstone for the mind. I agree with Tyrion. And look at you! You are reading a book! Well done.

If only maintaining your blade was that simple. Careful bladesmiths also pay close attention to the condition of the handle and fittings of the blade to ensure optimal performance and avoid breakage. So, how can you do the same for your mind?

Let me give you my top three:

1. **Choose a brain hobby.** Ideally, you want to have at least three hobbies: one to keep you physically active, one to keep you mentally active, and one to keep you socially active. If you can find one hobby that does all three, great! When it comes to staying mentally active, you want to choose a hobby that sits at the intersection of fun and intellectually challenging. Maybe you enjoy creative activities such as crafting new recipes or building things with Legos. Or perhaps you are more into puzzles or solving Sudoku problems. These sorts of activities give our brains something stimulating to work on, and just like with physical fitness your brain will rise to meet the challenge. Many of us play video games, which can be a great way to keep your mind active – as long as you are challenged in some way. Games that are passive or too easy might be enjoyable but typically lack the sort of intellectual stimulation needed to justify them as brain hobbies.

2. **Meditate and be mindful.** One of you just rolled your eyes, I can sense it. At face value, meditation and mindfulness seem like a luxurious waste of time. When I think about meditation, an image of a Buddhist monk sitting cross-legged and humming "ohm" comes to mind. Although some people are able to use that form of mindful meditation, there are other ways of doing it. Meditation is all about quieting the mind and being present. So, the key to effective meditation is finding an activity that lets you do just that. My meditation is weightlifting. I call it my iron asylum, my sanctum of sweat, my refuge of getting huge. When I

lift weights, my mind lets go of my worries and stress for a moment to focus on the task at hand. Find an activity that lets you clear the bustle of your cognitions and find a moment of peace and give yourself time to do it as often as possible.

3. **Read and write.** Thank you, Lord Tyrion, for your wisdom. Reading and writing have consistently been found to be some of the most effective ways to keep your mind active and help stave off issues like dementia and Alzheimer's disease. You do not need to be publishing books or reading a novel a day, any amount helps. Sometimes you can start small, such as turning on the subtitles while you watch television. Or, you can create a one-liner journal that sums up each day with a single sentence.

Structuring your day to include brain-friendly activities takes some effort, but the results are well worth it. Test these things out and discover what works best for you, and you are well on your way to maintaining your edge.

Improving Your Blade

You have learned how to mend and maintain your intellectual blade, but why stop there? Even the most intricate and well-honed swords could be improved and sharpened. Maintain a growth mindset and see yourself as a beautiful work in progress.

Psychologists rarely see people who are fully satisfied with their lives, and so there is not much research about pushing yourself beyond the basics of being mentally healthy. This means that the world of psychological improvement is an open field of possibilities. Here are a few ideas to get you started:

1. **Learn new skills.** Despite years of neuropsychological study, we still do not know exactly how much the brain can retain. The human mind is a seemingly endless memory drive that yearns to be filled with new abilities and ideas. Learning a new skill is a great way to dive into new interests and hobbies while also giving you opportunities to meet new people. If you do not know how to cook, try your hand at some simple recipes! If you

aren't sure how to fix that hole in your workout shorts, learn how to sew! The world is your oyster, and you can learn how to shuck it.

2. **Find sources of inspiration.** Look for new ways to learn and be inspired. Listen to a new genre of music. Go for a random drive in the countryside. Eat a weird brand of cheese. Attend a new church or social event. Watch some TEDx videos on YouTube. Talk about aliens with your neighbor. Our world is chock full of inspirational beauty and infinite sources of information. Be curious, and never stop searching.

3. **Share your ideas with others.** As you master the arts of repairing, maintaining, and improving your intellectual self, do not keep it a secret! Share your wisdom with the world. You could create a website about self-care, or write an article for the newspaper, or even present your thoughts at a university or a church. Teaching is an excellent way to learn and think creatively about your ideas.

Your mind is a beautiful thing. At times you will feel broken or bent out of shape, and that is okay. There is always room to repair, grow, and reach new heights.

Social: Keep Your Boat Afloat

Idaho is the invisible middle child of the United States.

People only know Idaho for her potatoes and hyper-conservative White people. But Idaho has more to offer than that: crystalline rivers, serene mountain ranges, and massive lakes. My family owned a tiny motorboat, and once in a while we would take off on a Saturday to go boating and fishing on the lake.

Boating is such a freeing experience. You glide across the glassy water and soak in the thick forestry and diverse animal life that surround most Idaho lakes. As fun as it was to go on these trips, we often had issues with our boat. Sometimes the motor would have issues, other times the boat developed a leak.

Boats are needy, you see. They require a bit more maintenance and use than other recreational vehicles. Although every boat is different, most boats need to be taken out on the water regularly.

You are not a boat, though. Perhaps you identify as a boat, but my guess is that most of you do not. However, your social life is kind of like a boat. Social activities can be just as freeing as an Idahoan boat ride - unless, of course, you have boat troubles.

Similarly, keeping a social life afloat is a lot like keeping a boat in prime condition. You have to use it often enough to keep things active, pay attention to leaks and cracks, and check the motor regularly.

Keep the Boat Active

The best way to keep your social life afloat and vibrant is to use it. You have to be engaging your social skills on a regular basis to avoid getting rusty. With great rust comes great social anxiety. Each time you get out there and do social things you will get better, no matter how rusty you might feel, but you have to take that brave step of launching your boat.

For many of us, this is easier said than done. Motivating yourself can be a real pain (which I why I cover that in our next chapter), but even the smallest attempts can make a big difference. Set a goal today to try one new social thing every week for the next month. Write it down on your calendar and try to start an activity streak by marking a star or check mark for each day of success. If you have a smartphone, set calendar reminders to help you stay on track. Accountability can be an excellent source of motivation.

Spend time with friends and loved ones. Spend time in safe public places and try making small talk with people you don't know. Go to a fast food restaurant and order something inside. All of these things will allow you to connect with others, flex your social muscles, and knock off some of that rust.

Watch for Leaks

Obviously, the worst part of boating is when the boat sinks. Most boats do not suddenly drop beneath the surface, though. You usually notice puddles or small streams begin to leak in through the bottom as soon as you get the boat on the water. If you do not keep the boat very active, there might be many leaks that need repairing. Or, you might accidentally hit a rock or log and instantly put the ship in jeopardy.

Our relationships are similar. Despite our best efforts to steer clear of conflict, any relationship that means something is bound to have ruptures. We will talk a lot more about how to handle these ruptures in Part 2, and so for now your task is simple. Consider the common causes of leaks in your social boat. Do you tend to let it sit inactively, only to realize there are holes in the relationship when you try to reach out and reconnect? Do you tend to get into arguments over little things like Marvel versus DC, or Yankees versus Red Sox? Do you accidentally hurt people's feelings, possibly in the attempt to be humorous or playful?

These are all natural parts of life and friendship. We get busy with our lives and lose touch with one another. Friendships begin to fade, and shared activities become less enjoyable. We also have diverse interests and we disagree from time to time. Sometimes we say stupid crap without thinking. And that is okay. We come with these quirks for a reason.

Think about the ways that these things may prevent you from sailing into the horizon with relationships. Although we cannot hope always to avoid relational leaks, we can try harder to control the boat.

Check the Motor

Motor issues are also common when boating. Sometimes things seem great until you get out on the water, only to realize you are out of gasoline or the propeller is missing. Although you do not need a motor to go boating per se, it sure helps get the boat moving.

Regarding your social life, your motor is the thing that motivates you towards relationship. This is the "why" for your decision to seek friendship and find belonging. Most of us have some motivation to engage socially, but sometimes those motivations are insufficient.

Think about what drove you to read this book. Think about the moments when you have felt hungry for one of the five essential food groups of friendship. The discomfort of isolation and the yearning for deeper connection and belonging can help energize you to take action. Many of us feel tempted to numb those feelings with junk food, television, or video games, but these are temporary solutions to a greater need for relationship.

Maintaining a satisfying social life isn't just about having friends.

After all, your health is at stake.

People who are socially active, even in small ways, tend to live longer and have decreased risk of developing depression, anxiety, and other mental health issues. Keep your boat active and well-tended to, and reap the rewards of a happier and safer ride.

Spiritual: Find Your True North

Spiritual health does not have to be about, or even include, religious beliefs.

Think of spirituality as your internal compass, the thing that gives you hope and keeps you moving in the right direction. This is about what you value, what you believe, and how you want to be remembered.

As a therapist, I constantly work with people who feel "lost," "stuck," or "confused." Feelings like these stem from living life against one's values. You can significantly improve your wellbeing when you find direction and move closer to your values.

Let me tell you a story to help illustrate my point.

The night held a silent chill as shards of brilliant moonlight cut through the dense branches of the Sawtooth National Park. I lay beneath a shamble of logs and pine boughs held together with para-chute cord as I pulled my blanket in around my neck. It was the final part of my "Wilderness Survival" merit badge, the last one I needed to become an Eagle Scout.

Each scout must hike out into the wilderness for several miles, set a camp out using only simple tools, survive for 24 hours, and then find your way back.

For me, it was one of the longest nights of my life.

Every snapping twig was a hungry bear, and each fluttering leaf was a stalking wolf.

I just had to make it to eight o'clock. I checked my wristwatch every three minutes, begging it to go faster.

When the sun finally rose and I could make out my surroundings, I started packing. I could not wait to get off that mountain and onto my soft, bear-free bed back home. I checked to make sure I had everything. Water canteen? Check. Pocket knife? Check. Sleeping bag? Check. Compass?

Holy crap.

My mind raced as I frantically tore through my backpack. I used it to get out here, it had to be around here somewhere. Eight o'clock was fast approaching. If I did not make it back and my scout leaders had to come and save me, then this was all for nothing.

After checking my pack, digging through leaves, and scouring the area for over an hour, I slumped against a tree in despair. I was lost in the wilderness, too scared to feel ashamed. My heart wrenched as I realized that I had failed to accomplish what I set out to do in the first place.

As the tears began to roll, I let myself slide to a seat at the base of the tree. And then, I felt a sudden sharp pain in my thigh.

The stupid thing was in my pants pocket.

Fear instantly transformed into jubilation. Now that I had my com-pass, I still had a chance to do this thing.

Sometimes in life, we get lost. We forget about what matters to us. We find ourselves living in ways that bring us suffering and regret, rather than joy and prosperity.

Compasses are designed to help you find your direction. Spirituality does this, too. When you imagine the things that matter most to you and the life you want to live, consider this to be your true north. North on a compass is the starting point for making navigation decisions. Once you know where north is, you can adjust your trajectory and find your way.

So, how do you begin to find your true north? Ask yourself these four questions:

When you die, how will people remember you?

In the film *Gladiator*, General Maximus tells us that "what we do in life echoes in eternity." I believe this is a promise and a warning. None of us want to be remembered as being greedy, rude, or violent. Perhaps worse, none of us want to be forgotten. Each of us hopes to be remembered, particularly in a positive light.

Think about the life you are currently living. If you were to die suddenly, what might people say at your funeral? People might say you were a good kid, that you really loved reading books on friendship, and that you died too soon. But will they say the things you really want them to say?

"What an amazing friend!" "He came and visited me every day while I was in the hospital." "She listened to my problems and helped me get my life together." "She was so smart and funny, I loved her puns." "Dad was such a great man. He made me into the person I am today." "I'm really, really going to miss her."

Live your life knowing that your actions echo long after you are gone and know that you have the power to choose what memories echo the loudest. As you find your true north, those memories might be your intended destination.

What do you want in life?

This is more than just a bucket list.

All of us hope to live comfortably, travel the world, and have fun. Yet, life is more than earning big bucks and driving fancy cars. I used to work in an assisted living facility where I spent countless hours talking to folks who were at the end stages of life, many of whom were on their deathbeds. Those conversations completely changed my perspective on what matters in life. Dying people do not talk about how they wanted to have earned more money or bought bigger houses. Very few people lamented about not getting to go to Las Vegas or even Paris.

Each and every one of them wished they had spent more time with loved ones. More Christmases and Hanukkahs, more birthdays and road trips, and more boring Tuesday afternoons sitting on the back porch together.

You see, when people reach the sunset of life they often look back and think about love, connection, and belonging. Dying wouldn't be as scary if we knew we could still talk to our friends and family members. I believe that the greatest regret at the final destination is to look back and yearn for deeper connection.

Think about what matters most to you in life. What brings you joy and meaning? These experiences are what you hope to have along the journey to your final destination. Keep these things in mind when you find yourself straying away from your values.

What beliefs help you make sense of the universe?

I am a believer.

I believe in the boundless nature of reality. I believe that each of us is at the center of our own universe, and we so bravely adventure from birth into the mysterious depths of death because we have hope. I believe that, no matter how chaotic and random the cosmos may be, each of us has a significant part to play. Terrible things will happen to wonderful people, and wonderful things will happen to terrible people. Despite our feeble capacity to control the world around us, we do have the power to author our own stories.

I believe in an infinitely loving creator of our plane of existence. I believe that this God as we have named has programmed the fabric of reality for some unknowable purpose. Like an archeologist brushing off an interminable artifact, we can uncover God's mysteries through science and exploration.

Oh, and I super believe in aliens. They are out there, I just know it.

Compasses are less useful when you have absolutely no idea where you are. If you were dropped off in the middle of some strange desert, you might not know whether to head north or west to find the nearest village.

Think about your beliefs about the world and how it works. Some of us have religious beliefs that help keep our compass well oriented. Others might have morals learned through life lessons, good parenting, or mentorship. These beliefs help us keep things in perspective and remind us who we are and where we should head.

What makes the world a better place?

Since the dawn of pain and hurt, we have brought suffering to one another. Wars and feuds and senseless bickering fuel a never-ending chain of caustic rage and revenge. I believe that our purpose in the universe is to make it better. We can always make it better. The purest and most craved gift is love, and so we lock it away for safe keeping. When we open our hearts and offer the warm embrace of belonging, this little speck of dust called Earth becomes just a bit brighter.

Yet, contrary to the gospel according to *The Beetles*, we need more than love. Humor, excitement, good food, cat pictures, and Frank's Red Hot Sauce certainly make the world a better place, too.

Each of us can use our skills and talents to improve the world in some way. As you learn how to apply these for the betterment of society, you start to move in the direction your compass is pointing. You might be good at taking phone calls from friends in moments when they feel overwhelmed. You might cook a mean pot of chili. You might be good at smiling and thanking the cashier. No matter how small, you can do your part to make the world a better place.

Your spiritual compass can help you move forward in life when you feel lost or stuck. Give yourself time to check in with your compass. Your values may change on your journey. You might find it helpful to write down your answers to those four questions and reevaluate from time to time.

Chapter Summary

Personal health and self-care are of the utmost importance for being a good friend. As we learn to be physically healthy, we have more energy and longevity to engage in a fruitful relationship. Psychological wellbeing gives us an edge in everyday life and helps us survive tumultuous times. In addition to keeping our relationships afloat, our social lives also help to fortify health and wellness. And finally, spirituality can help us stay on track when we feel lost and isolated. These four facets of healthy living allow us to put on our own oxygen masks so that we can more fully bring life into our relationships.

Questions to Ponder:

- What areas of your self-care do you tend to neglect?

- Do any of these areas come easier than others? Why or why not?

- Who in your life do you think could help you work on one or more of these areas of self-care?

CHAPTER 7
PULLING THE TOOTH

I remember when I got my first loose tooth.

Naturally, this was the end for kindergarten Kyler.

Loose teeth are the equivalent of getting your first grey hairs in middle adulthood. My tooth was falling out, and I was dying. I wandered around the house sobbing because I would soon have a gaping hole in my handsome smile. I begged my mom to let me stay home from school. I wouldn't touch or wiggle it or anything. I would just stare at it in the mirror, begging it to go back to normal.

It didn't work.

After a few weeks of babying my baby tooth, things got worse. I couldn't eat anything crunchy or sticky. The darned thing would flutter when I talked. Boy, did it hurt. My parents offered to help me pull it out, but I wouldn't even let them get close enough to look. After much coaxing and promising of reward from the tooth fairy, I agreed to let my dad pull it out. I tied dental floss around this tiny symbol of my immortal childhood and handed the other end to my dad. He looked me in the eye and said "Okay, this isn't going to hurt a bit, it's barely in there. On the count of three." He started the countdown.

"One."

"Tw–"

I changed my mind.

As I began to scream "NO WAIT," I jerked my head away.

The line tightened, and my tooth popped right out.

Even when we recognize the loose teeth in our lives, we sometimes go to great lengths to avoid pulling them out. We fear the pain and the potential consequences. We fear admitting that the tooth is loose in the first place. We fear judgment and being seen as less-than.

You have traveled many chapters to get here. We have learned about schemas, relational needs, attachment, defenses, and self-care. My hope is that these lessons helped you to see yourself and find acceptance. You may have seen some things that you would like to change. But change is not always easy. Old habits die hard, and sometimes we prefer to leave it be.

You picked up this book for a reason. Part of you wants to make changes for the better, even if it means facing some discomfort. This chapter is all about learning how to make those changes.

Depending on which therapist you ask, therapy is all about making your life better. You get to learn new things about yourself, understand who you are as a person, and learn new skills and ideas that help bolster your quality of life. This book is designed to help you do some of these things on your own, but sometimes it helps to get help.

Change is not easy. People make changes every day without going to therapy. And you can, too. Here are the steps:

Step One: Accept the Tooth

You are awesome.

And, you have some loose teeth.

Each of us is perfectly imperfect. When we signed up to be human, it was a package deal. We came with abilities and assets as well as flaws and foibles. If each of us were perfect, we would all be the same. And we would all have muscles like Dwayne "The Rock" Johnson.

This is not the world we live in. We live in a world where people come in different shapes and sizes and share unique ideas and worldviews. Despite having eight billion people on our little planet, no two of us are the same. And each of us is worthy of love and belonging. Yes, even the ones that put pineapple on pizza.

As you read through these first few chapters, you may have noticed some things about yourself that get between you and friendship. You may have noticed some deadly schemas hanging over your head, you may have realized how your attachment style has affected your relationships, or perhaps you noticed some relational barriers that keep you from sharing your kingdom. It may be that self-care and prioritizing your health will be the first step, just like putting on your own oxygen mask.

Your first task is to accept these issues as part of the human condition. Think of yourself in the context of your life. You are the way that you are because of your history, your genetic code, your experiences, and your environment. And, you are also this way because of the choices you have made along the way. We cannot change your history or your genetics, at least not yet, but we can change our thoughts and behaviors. But first, we have to accept that something needs to change.

Step Two: Experience the Toothache

We tend to react with worry, anger, or sadness when we notice things about ourselves that we do not like. So, what do we do when we feel that way? We avoid or numb the discomfort by pushing the thoughts away, distracting ourselves with video games or Netflix, or smothering the negativity with piles of junk food.

The avoidance of these uncomfortable feelings causes a nasty chain of events. First, our brains learn that the avoidance is preferred and pleasurable. Playing Candy Crush is much nicer than thinking about how lonely I feel. So, my brain motivates me when I avoid thinking about my problem by rewarding me when I play Candy Crush.

Over time, this becomes a habit. My problem continues to wiggle like a loose tooth, but I choose to distract myself rather than pay attention to my issues. At some point, the problem gets in the way of something valuable. Interpersonal barriers may keep potential friends from connecting with me. Deadly schemas may discourage me from being social at a party. I sit in the corner by the chip bowl, anxious and alone.

Ouch.

Suddenly, I am experiencing the hurt of my loose tooth. Past behavior is the best predictor of future behavior, and so my habits of avoidance send me back to the rewardingly numb land of Candy Crush. This choice gives me short-term relief from the problem, but the problem remains.

Every human emotion has a purpose, even the uncomfortable ones.

The pain of having a loose tooth motivates us to act. Our bodies know that something in the mouth is not working quite right, that something hurts, and that we need to fix it. At the moment of hurt, we have a choice. We can avoid the pain, avoid touching the soreness of the tooth, or we can do something about it.

Let the discomfort fuel your actions and give you energy for change.

Step Three: Make a Game Plan

Take a good hard look at what you would like to change, embrace the motivation that comes with discomfort and desire, and turn it into an actionable goal.

The secret to setting a good goal is simple: avoid dead man goals.

If a dead person can achieve your primary goal, it's not a great goal. Dead people can lose weight. Dead people can eat less junk food. Dead people can spend less time playing video games.

Change your language from subtraction to addition. In other words, instead of trying to restrict yourself from doing something, try to add more of the opposite. For example, instead of eating less junk food, you might want to try eating more vegetables. Or, instead of spending less time playing video games, try spending more time in the common room of your dormitory.

Set goals that give you more in life, not less.

Step Four: Pull the Tooth

You have noticed the thing you want to change and accepted it. You have felt the pain and discomfort of missed opportunities and lost relationships. You are motivated, and now you are ready to address this thing.

Time to pull the tooth.

And just like pulling teeth, making lifestyle changes can be difficult. Here are some ways to make it easier:

Break it Down

If you were asked to move an entire house from one end of the street to the other, how would you do it?

You probably wouldn't walk up to the side of the house, get a firm grip on the foundation, and heave for all you are worth. Well, you might, but I doubt it would work. Instead, after you ice your back, you might take the house apart brick by brick until you run out of bricks, and then move on to the roofing, and so on and so forth, until nothing remains. It would take a long time, but you could do it.

The same is true when we set goals for ourselves. The task may feel overwhelming, more difficult even than moving a house by hand. But when we break down insurmountable tasks into many smaller tasks, things start to look surmountable.

Think about the thing you want to change. Now, break that thing down into bite-sized pieces. Here is an example. Let's say you would like to start being more sociable. You could break that down into at least five pieces: spending time around others, making small talk, sharing stories about yourself, making eye contact, and reading body language. Next, pick one thing to focus on. Just one. Dedicate all of your focus on that until it becomes easy, and then move on to the next. If you come across something that never seems to get easier, it is time to break it down again.

Maintain a growth mindset, and you will move this house.

Make it Fun

The absolute worst part of being an athlete was the conditioning.

Coaches typically add some form of extra exercise called conditioning to the end of every practice. Most of the time, this meant doing a few laps or sprints. These extra exercises were used to help us reach optimal fitness for competition. Football conditioning was the most punishing, running around in the blazing heat while donned in a plastic helmet shell and thick heavy padding. If it weren't for my cravings for the sweet, sweet feeling of smashing into someone while running at a full sprint, I would have never stuck with football.

Although conditioning was downright awful, my coaches found ways to make it fun. Sometimes we would have competitions to see who could run the fastest or do the most pushups. Other times we would break into groups to do relay races or obstacle courses. The fun got us through the difficulty of conditioning, and it can help you pull your tooth.

Find ways to make the change enjoyable. This might require some creativity. For example, if you are trying to spend more time in social situations you might buy yourself a favorite snack to take with you and share with others. Or, if you are trying to exercise more often you might try listening to exciting or upbeat music when you go to work out. Over time, your brain will learn to associate fun and pleasure with these new behaviors, which helps to cement changes that last.

Enlist Help

Think back to the moving a house metaphor. Things would be much easier if you asked for help, right? When the task feels too much for one person, you will want to build up a team of supports that can keep you on track towards your goal.

Asking for help is not always easy. Start with someone you trust, someone who understands your situation and wants to help you towards your goal. This may be a teacher, a friend, a mentor, a parent, or a therapist, for example. Tell them your goal and ask them for any ideas they might have to help you reach it. You can also ask them to check in or bug you about your goal periodically.

Help does not have to be a person, although people are preferable. Your smartphone can become the fifth lobe of your brain if you use it properly. Set calendar reminders to go to the coffee shop and meet new people. Use fitness apps to track your intake and activity levels. Put a motivational image as your phone wallpaper to act as a constant reminder of your goal.

Bonus Step: The Checkup

Congrats! Now you have a game plan for addressing the change you want to make in your life.

A few words of caution: do not let the change fade over time. You worked too hard to get to this point. Just like with proper dental hygiene, each of us should schedule regular checkups. Find ways to check in with yourself after you reach your goal to make sure you stay on track. Too many of us are guilty of the New Year's resolution check-in, where we sink into a deep depression because we see little or lost progress towards last year's goals.

Some people might find it helpful to use a consistent deadline, something that you already have to keep track of like rent or at the end of each season. Do what works best for you, but make sure it happens often. A good rule of thumb is to schedule the checkup more often after first meeting a goal and then gradually allowing more time to pass if everything is satisfactory.

Chapter Summary

Making lasting lifestyle changes can be incredibly difficult. You need a game plan to help strategize your approach and keep you on track. First, you must compassionately accept your problem as part of the human condition. Next, you must allow yourself the discomfort that the problem brings and transform it into an actionable goal. Finally, you must make progress through strategy, consistency, and persistence. You've got this.

Questions to Ponder:

- Have you had to make significant life changes before? What helped you pull it off? What was unhelpful, or created setbacks?

- Do you have a mentor to help you reach your goals? If not, who in your life might be willing to help out?

PART 2
LOOKING OUTWARD

College freshmen learn how to do all sorts of things.

How to buy vegetables, how to cut your own hair without looking like a rave DJ, how to use one side of the towel for your face and the other side for your butt, and how to try new things, for better or for worse.

The year was 2010. The time, two o'clock in the morning. The place, my dorm room. I was cramming furiously for a midterm exam. My headphones were blasting some righteous dubstep to drown out the sounds of the cicadas outside my window. Suddenly, I felt a tap on my shoulder.

"Hey Kyler, want to go for a Steak 'n Shake run?"

One of my buddies, Steven, and a group of other students were headed on a late-night food quest.

"Um…"

I really didn't want to. Who were those other guys? What is a Steak 'n Shake?

But then I remembered I wanted to make friends. "Sure." Studying could wait.

My roommate BJ was also awake. His earphones were turned up so loud that I didn't need to see his screen to know he was watching *Jersey Shore*.

As soon as Steven and his crew started to leave, I felt something strange. My heart wrenched. My throat tightened up into a knot. What was wrong with me?

I felt bad about leaving dear BJ by himself, uninvited.

In the great search for human connection, we often leave people behind. In Part 1 you learned how to improve your capacity for friendship. However, your interpersonal skills and insights can only take you so far when you are unable or unwilling reach out and apply them to the relationship. This is what Part 2 is all about.

"Hey, BJ," I waved to get his attention.

"What?" He sounded irritated.

"Steven and the gang are going out for Steak 'n Shake, want to come along?"

"SURE!"

I'm still not sure if he was excited to join or glad to turn off his show. Regardless, we were able to enjoy BJ's company and he ours. By inviting others to join us at the table of friendship, we provide opportunities for sorts of belonging we so profoundly crave for ourselves.

Looking outward is all about bringing your insight and interpersonal skills to others, reaching out, and being mindful of the dos and don'ts of friendship.

Think of it this way. A gardener may have great awareness about themselves and toil endlessly to help their flowers grow. Yet, the plants will not prosper unless the gardener promotes their growth through proper love and care. Learn how to look outward and notice the mistakes of friendship, and your chances of growing one will become stronger.

CHAPTER 8
THE SAVED SEAT

A long, long time ago in a cafeteria far, far away, an eager Kyler went to lunch on his first day of middle school.

They were serving pizza *and* hamburgers, a steadfast offering before the time of First Lady Michelle Obama and her diabetes prevention programs.

I remember grabbing my tray, loading it up with happiness, and then realizing I needed to find somewhere to sit. My dollar store sneakers squeaked nervously as I walked along the aisles of tables filled with fellow acne-ridden pseudo-adults. Some avoided eye contact, others gave me a subtle head shake to signal that I should keep moving. I found a table that was mostly sparse and prepared to settle in for some greasy goodness when the kid on my right set their hand down on the bench.

"Nope, this seat is saved."

I know, this is a fairly cliché memory. But many of you know it all too well.

Oh, the rejection, oh, the hurt. Someone far more valuable than I was destined to take this place of belonging.

Most of us do not want to inflict those feelings on others. I would argue that those who do have also felt the sting of loneliness. Some of us react like the Hen of attachment, safeguarding our relationships by keeping outsiders at bay.

Although most of us no longer venture the halls of the cafeteria, all of us want a seat at the table of relationship.

The best friends learn not to save seats for one another, but to bring more chairs.

This chapter is all about learning how to find and create space for belonging.

Creating space for the relationship is a lot like hosting a party. You might send out **invitations** so that others know they are welcome to join. You would also need to find a good **time** to get everyone together, and once people arrive, you would want the partygoers to feel **engaged** and entertained. The same is true for friendship.

Invitation

Rather than investing all of your energy searching for a seat, the best way to avoid being alone at the table of relationship is to invite others to join you.

Find ways to invite others into your life. This doesn't necessarily mean inviting people to hang out, although those sorts of invites are helpful. Even small interpersonal invitations, or bids for connection, can help others feel welcome when they are around you. Asking someone about their weekend allows them some space to talk about themselves and feel heard by someone else. Offering to buy your coworker a snack on your way to the vending machine lets them know that you keep them in mind. These invitations for connection help let others know that they matter to you and that you are open to their friendship.

There are so many ways to send invitations for deeper connection, but here are a few ideas to get you started:

1. **Bring a buddy.** If you already have one or two people you spend time with, try inviting new people to join in on the fun. You might invite a random classmate to join you and your friend for lunch, or perhaps you could ask another couple to join you and your romantic partner on a double date. Sometimes it is easier to accept an invitation when we know there will be others there as well.

2. **Invite the stranger.** Sometimes we avoid spending time with people we don't know very well. This creates a problem, as you have to spend time together to transform a stranger into a not-so-stranger. You never know who you might connect with, and sometimes friendship comes from strange places.

3. **Host an event.** If you have the time and resources to host a get-together, this is the top tier of invitations. You might invite some of your neighbors to a barbecue or to watch *The Oscars* together at your house. You could keep it small and ask a few people to join you at a local pub or pizza place to eat and play a new board game. By hosting events and encouraging others to join, you are communicating investment in shared friendship experiences.

Time

Life tends to keep us busy. We all have bills to pay, classes to attend, and various responsibilities to keep us occupied. Sometimes, people will not have time to come to the party.

However, many of us become so absorbed in our day-to-day obligations that we do not allow sufficient time for relationship. If your day is jam-packed with work, meals, and sleep, you won't have time for friends. Similarly, other people may be too busy with their lives to spend time with us.

Think of setting aside time as providing space at the table of relationships. In the pursuit of connection, look for people who are willing to make the time to be in relationships. They say that time is money, but what they mean is time is value. We spend time on the things that matter to us. People who do not have time for relationships may not value them as much as other things.

We cannot control how much time others are willing to spend, but we can find ways to be ready when we want to spend time on relationships. Here are a few ways you can do that:

1. **Pick your top five.** Many of us have too many things to worry about. Everything from surviving at work to writing your next

killer tweet will sap time and energy from your week. Warren Buffet is famous for telling people to stop trying to prioritize or manage too many things, and just pick five. Take a moment to think about all of the things that matter in your life. You might think of things like your health, family, faith, financial security, and friendship. Pick the five most important things that you cannot live happily without and stop worrying about the rest. Prioritize your time and energy on those five things, and you will notice how much easier it is to find time for what matters most.

2. **Set a consistent schedule.** If your week is constantly changing or your sleep schedule is off, you are going to struggle to find time for other people. Want to hang out next weekend? You don't know, because next weekend is going to be another day of disorganized chaos. School and work can only take up so much time, and you do not want to wait to graduate or retire to start living. Set a consistent schedule that effectively allows you to meet your top five priorities and stick to it.

3. **Learn to say "no."** Remember, time is valuable. People are always going to ask for your time and energy. The temptation is to be generous and offer it freely, but this comes with consequences. As we continue to agree to meet the needs of bosses, teachers, siblings, and parents, we sacrifice time that could be spent on our top five. Saying "no" is actually a way for you to say "yes" to the things that matter most.

Engagement

People may take the time to come to your party, but if they do not feel engaged or entertained, they might lose interest. The gathering might feel cold or awkward, and people may not want to talk to one another. Everyone gathers around the chips and dip, eats, and then leaves.

You might have made space at the table of friendship, but those who join may feel unwanted or unwelcome. There are many ways to keep others involved, but here are a few tips to get you started:

1. **Be curious.** Find ways to be curious about the people around you. Every one of us has a story to tell, memories to share, and unique beliefs and interests. We love television series like *Friends* and *How I Met Your Mother* because even though we see the same few characters in every episode, there are always new discoveries to be made. The people around you are more than just your classmates, coworkers, and cashiers. Ask good, open-ended questions that provide opportunities for others to share about themselves. You never know who might end up being a great friend.

2. **Use tasteful humor.** If we have learned anything from Dr. Patch Adams, it is that laughter really is the best medicine. People love to laugh, and when we are able to provide a healthy dose of humor, we breathe life into our interactions. Comedy is a double-edged blade, though, as our words might be insensitive or hurtful to others. Stick to wholesome jokes that are respectful to identity markers such as ethnicity, religion, neurodiversity, and gender. Learning how to be funny takes time, but I believe in you.

3. **Pay a compliment.** Everyone loves a nice compliment. When you compliment someone on their new t-shirt or on how amazing their speech was, you are pointing out the value that you see in others. This helps other people feel recognized and welcome in your company. If you compliment something they value about themselves, they will also begin to see you as a person with good taste.

Each of us can provide places for belonging for others. As you learn to create space for friendship, others will be drawn to your table.

I love pie. I love it very much. But, love is not a pie, bound by the limits of its slices. Love is an endless fountain of pie-flavored goodness that can be infinitely shared with others. If everyone freely shared their friendship, we wouldn't need to save seats.

Chapter Summary

We live in a world where people continuously face exclusion and rejection. Luckily, each of us has the power to create space for friendship and belonging. By inviting others to join us, prioritizing our relationships, and helping others feel welcome, we can help others experience the connection that we ourselves crave.

Questions to Ponder:

- What tends to hold you back from inviting others into your life?

- Who in your life do you think feels excluded or ignored by others? How might you extend connection to them?

- Who do you feel does a good job at helping others feel like they belong?

CHAPTER 9
NINE FRIENDSHIP FOLLIES

"Everybody makes mistakes

Everybody has those days

Everybody knows what, what' I'm talkin' 'bout

Everybody gets that way"

The gospel, according to Miley Cyrus.

We humans are perfectly imperfect. And sometimes, we say or do things that are just downright stupid. Making mistakes in relationships is just part of life's package deal.

That being said, imperfection does not mean permission to do all of the stupid things. Humans have these amazing organs called "brains" that we sometimes use to control our behaviors and reduce the likelihood of making mistakes.

A fancy word for a mistake is "folly," which actually has two meanings. Folly means to make a foolish mistake or fail to plan ahead, but it can also mean to engage in a costly but ultimately fruitless endeavor.

When it comes to friendship, there are a few things that can damage the quality of the relationship – or end it entirely. If you are reading this book in the hope of finding friendship, we would both be remiss if you spent all of this time and energy only to make a mistake that ruined a perfectly good relationship.

The best way to prevent a friendship folly is to be aware of common mishaps and plan ahead. By learning about the mistakes many people make, you can avoid following in their footsteps.

Friendship Folly #1: Jealousy

A study from 2018 published in *Science Advances* found that men and women tend to try to date people that they estimate to be about 25% more desirable than themselves. I think this might also be true when it comes to friendship. We want to be friends with people who are funny, creative, or smart because they bring a little something extra to the relationship.

The catch is that sometimes we become jealous of the things our friends have that we do not. We feel envious when they get to go on cool vacations and when they get promotions at work. We feel a bit green when they find new friends and spend time with others. It isn't because we do not want them to have joy and happiness. It is because most friendships tend to be fairly egalitarian, or equal. When our friends get the things we want, we feel jealous because we see feel we should get the same, that we deserve equal treatment.

Feelings of jealousy are perfectly normal. This is your brain's way of telling you that you want something that you are missing. However, when we act on these feelings, we tend to do it in ways that damage the relationship. We withdraw and begin to distance ourselves from our friends. We lash out in hurt and anger when our friends merely want to share the joy of their success.

When we begin to feel jealous of our friends, we must fight back against feeling less-than. Celebrate with your friends just as you would hope they might cheer for you in your success.

Friendship Follies #2 and #3: Selfishness and Selflessness

Did you know that a group of crabs is called a cast?

Apparently, when fishermen catch a cast of crabs, they can put them together in a container without a lid. Why? Because every time one of the crabs gets close to escaping, the other crabs will grab it and try to pull themselves up with it, resulting in the escapee crab being pulled back down with the rest of them. The selfishness of the cast keeps the crabs in captivity.

If the crabs learned how to boost one another up, take turns climbing, and look out for the cast, they could escape together. Similarly, when we only look out for ourselves, our friendships take the toll.

Sometimes our friends will ask for some of our time and energy to help meet their needs. They might ask us to help them move out of their apartment or to loan them a few dollars for lunch. Obviously, we would rather use our free time to relax and use our money to buy things for ourselves, but friendship calls for some sacrifice.

And yet, we must also look out for ourselves. Many of us, myself included, are far too quick to give everything we have to our friends out of fear of loss. We would rather give up every weekend of the year to help our friends move than risk losing those friendships.

This sort of selflessness comes with a price. Our friends might begin to believe that we unlimited resources to give. We give up what time and energy we might need to maintain our health and sanity because we think our friends need it more. Find balance between selflessness and selfishness. Your friends love you for who you are, not for what you give them.

Friendship Folly #4: Ulterior Motives

The year was 1998 when my parents bought our first video game console, The Super Nintendo. It came with the holy trinity of games: The Legend of Zelda: A Link to the Past, Super Mario World, and Donkey Kong Country.

Each day of my seven-year-old existence was dedicated to getting my hands on that knobby little grey controller. My parents used this to their advantage by putting in place a token economy. I could earn "Kid Bucks" by doing chores and getting good grades, which I could then turn around and spend on screen time.

Eventually, I learned a way around their system. Screen time was expensive at home. But, if I went over to other kids' houses, I could play as much as I wanted - for free. I began scouting out kids at school that were lucky enough to have video games *and* parents who were willing to let them play as much as they wanted.

The problem was, none of those friendships lasted. I would get in a few playdates, glue myself to their television, and ignore the potential friend entirely.

When friendships are made in the hopes of gaining something other than connection and belonging, we set a weak foundation for the relationship to build on. All of us are guilty of starting relationships with ulterior motives, such as getting a job, making someone jealous, making our parents happy, or mooching off of their wealth. Focus on building friendships where the gain is having the other person in your life.

Friendship Folly #5: Lying

Lies are like the top half of a bag of potato chips, empty and disappointing.

When we lie to our friends, we attempt to cover up something in the relationship. Our deceit keeps our friends from realizing that we are stupid, weak, or unimportant. We say things like "I'm fine" when we actually feel like curling up and crying ourselves to sleep. We spin webs of excuses for why we can't help them do their landscaping. We tell them that they look great wearing their pants below their butt cheeks to show off their boxers.

Sometimes we lie with good intentions or tell small fibs, and like any friend would we tell them that their dress does not make them look fat. However, a friendship based on lies is as meaningful as an empty bag of chips. Find ways to be honest with your friends, particularly when it comes to self-disclosure. Your friends want to know how you really feel and what you really think, not what you think they want to hear.

Friendship Folly #6: Teasing

A guy I knew in high school typically greeted his friends by calling them unsavory words, the tamest perhaps being "loser face" and "fat piece of crap." His friends always laughed, and so he just kept doing it. Now, he isn't necessarily known for making and keeping friends, but this does go to show that teasing can happen in friendship.

We love teasing our friends and loved ones. Much like when kittens play together, a few paw swipes and ear bites can help keep things lively. Unfortunately, some of us take the teasing too far, or sometimes the teasing becomes central to the relationship.

If your relationship involves teasing, check in with the other person to see how your jests are received. Sometimes our friends worry they will upset us by pushing back or telling us the teasing is hurtful. And, if the relationship is mostly based on teasing, the friendship may have morphed into bullying. No one wants to be friends with bullies.

Friendship Folly #7: Exclusion

Once upon a time, I was the captain of my high school football team. Our little town was all about sports, so I was a bit of a local celebrity. Despite the popularity athleticism brought me, my success also earned me some disdain from my classmates.

I remember walking into History class one Friday, game day, when I overheard some of my classmates talking about an after-game party that was going to be held at one of my teammates' houses. Sweet! Tonight's game was a surefire win, and so it would be fun to join my teammates in some celebratory Guitar Hero and junk food. As I approached and took my seat, the conversation was hushed and abruptly ended. When I asked what they were talking about, they told me it was about the homework they forgot to do.

Exclusion is the executioner of relationship.

When we exclude others, we send messages of rejection, disapproval, and distrust.

Sadly, we exclude each other in more ways than withholding invitations. When we hide parts of our lives from one another and keep our friends out, we exclude them from sharing our experiences. We choose to present our best selves and hide our inner struggle to preserve the relationship. Find ways to invite others in, just as you would want to be invited.

Friendship Folly #8: Obsession

Have you ever gone a long time without drinking any water?

I remember the first hike I ever took to the top of The Seven Devils mountain range, some of the tallest peaks in Idaho. My fellow Boy Scouts and I set up base camp after hiking for several hours up into the maw of the park's sharp ridges and glacial lakes. It took us an entire day to get to base camp, and so we planned to continue on the next morning. The following day, we set off to conquer the highest peak, The He-Devil. After several hours of hiking, I had a sick realization.

I forgot my water bottle back at base camp.

I was way too proud to ask for a swig of someone else's canteen, and so I pressed onward for the remaining six hours of the climb. At some point, I stopped sweating and began to get light headed. All I could think about was water. When we got back to base camp, I furiously drank all the water I could find.

And then I puked.

I do not remember much from that oh so dry hike. I do not even recall the view from the top of The He-Devil. I was so obsessed with water that I forgot to enjoy the trip. And, I made the mistake of drinking so much that I ended up losing the water I needed.

Friends are awesome. So awesome, in fact, that you were willing to pick up a book about them. We yearn for belonging and connection just like we yearn for water on a long hike. However, sometimes this causes us to fixate on our friends when we finally have them. We smother our new friends with text messages, invitations to hang out, and questions about their lives to the point where a relational puke happens, and the friend creates distance for their sanity and safety.

The trick to rehydration after dehydration also works with relational obsession. You feel starved of the thing you need, and the temptation is to take in as much as you can while it lasts. Instead, you have to take small sips, send fewer texts, and ease into the relationship slowly.

Friendship Folly #9: Stagnation

Imagine that you and a friend meet up every single Tuesday to go out for lunch. You go to the same place, order the same food, and you talk about the same topics. You and your friend may feel a sense of belonging, and the relationship may help meet some of your needs for companionship, but ultimately nothing seems to change.

Stagnation happens when the relationship ceases to grow. We become complacent in our relationships, and we forget to look for new opportunities for fun and learning.

They say, "if it ain't broke, don't fix it," but I would argue that "just because it ain't broke, doesn't mean it's as good as it's gonna get."

Find ways to deepen and fortify your relationships. Try new things together, share new stories about yourself, and be curious. Your friendship is not a sink that needs fixing when it leaks. Your friendship is a garden that can always be enhanced with new plants, a sweet fountain, and a few butterflies.

As you learn to notice the follies of friendship, you will gain something that the captain of the Titanic did not: awareness. Do not allow your friendship to sink because of the human errs we make in relationships. Instead, find ways to sail on into the horizon to share greater adventures together.

Chapter Summary

We are all perfectly imperfect and prone to making mistakes. When it comes to the relationship, we tend to say or do things that unintentionally damage our connections with others. Our jealousy, selfishness, and exclusiveness can harm those we love. These mistakes, or follies, can be avoided if we know what to look out for.

Questions to Ponder:

- What follies are you most fond of? In other words, do any of these tend to get in the way of you and the relationships you want to have?

- Did you notice any themes of attachment in any of these follies?
- How can you avoid making old mistakes in your friendships?

CHAPTER 10
TEN FRIENDSHIP FORTIFIERS

I just do not understand why television commercials for beverages, like Sunny D, will say "fortified with vitamins and minerals" when describing their products.

Do they mean that their original product was weak, and so they added some stuff to help it be stronger? Do they mean that I will be stronger if I drink Sunny D? If so, shouldn't I be able to bench press a truck by now?

But I digress.

Chapter 9 was all about learning things to avoid, and in doing so, I gave you a bunch of dead person goals. Dead people can avoid acting out of envy. Dead people can avoid telling lies. And, as far as I know, dead people don't tease us too much.

Instead of giving you more dead person goals, his chapter is all about learning the things you should aspire for in friendship. These are the vitamins and minerals you want to add to your relationship to help keep it strong and healthy.

I present to you: *The Ten Friendship Fortifiers*.

Friendship Fortifier #1: Gratitude

Soon after I learned the words "mommy" and "daddy," my parents taught me how to say, "thank you." To this day, I am thankful.

Gratitude plays a critical role in our relationships. Words of thanks communicate a recognition of sacrifice from the other and a sense of value for the shared connection.

Unfortunately, we sometimes miss the mark in providing a sufficient expression of gratitude. Sometimes we expect a bit more than the words "thank you" after helping our buddy carry his piano up three flights of stairs. Sometimes we need to express gratitude for small things, like being there to talk in a time of need or offering to help out with the dishes. Aim to make your expressions of gratitude to be just a bit more what your friends provide for you. You are telling them "thank you" for more than just their actions, but also the relationship you share.

Here are a few simple ways to integrate gratitude into your friendship:

1. **Practice saying "thank you" as part of your goodbye.** This might feel silly but try telling your friends thank you when you are done interacting or hanging out. "Thank you for being my friend" sends the message that you appreciate the relationship and the time you spent together.

2. **Notice the small things.** Try to notice the smaller, less obvious things your friends do for you. Some friends will try to make you laugh or smile when you feel down. Some friends may always bring you a soda during your gaming sessions. When you notice these little gestures of friendship, notice it and express appreciation.

3. **Return the favor.** Find ways to equally do for your friends what they have done for you. If your friend buys you lunch, return the favor by buying next time. If the favor is something that cannot be returned or reciprocated (i.e., if your friend helps you move into a new apartment), find some way to express your thanks. A good rule of thumb is to consider what it would cost to hire a stranger to help you with the favor and try to reimburse your friend accordingly.

Friendship Fortifier #2: Being Proud

Pride is a controversial word, particularly in Christian circles. Pride cometh before the fall. But I believe that pride can be used for good, too.

Fred Rogers, of *Mr. Rogers' Neighborhood,* was known not just for his skill as a puppeteer and actor, but for his outstanding sense of humanity and compassion. A book called *I am Proud of You: My Friendship with Fred Rogers* talks about the incredible inspiration and encouragement he gave to others by using five simple words:

"I am proud of you."

When we are proud of our friends, we shine a beacon onto the significance of their feats and their worth as a person. Many of us struggle to see value in ourselves and the work we do, and our friends can help with that. Remember how awesome you felt when your parents proudly displayed your first drawing on the kitchen fridge. Find ways to express your pride for those around you. Here are a few ideas to get you started:

1. **Brag about your friends.** When your friend does something awesome, tell other people about it. Chances are, those people will congratulate them in person or via social media. Make sure that your brags are in good taste. Avoid talking up feats that your friend may want to keep private. If in doubt, ask your friend's permission to brag (which is, in itself, a way to show pride).

2. **Show up for things.** If your friend receives an award, is featured in a play, or is hosting a party, make sure to be there. Your presence during important events shows pride and support for what they do. If you cannot attend, let your friends know you wished you could be there and find ways to make it up to them.

3. **Use Mr. Rogers' magic.** Say the words "I am proud of you." These five simple words carry so much wholesome power. Tell your friends how proud you are of who they are and what they have accomplished.

Friendship Fortifier #3: Advocacy

At the meeting of Rivendell, the fellowship of the ring is assembled as people come to Frodo's aid. You have my sword, my bow, my axe.

Nothing feels better than when someone has your back.

A significant driver in our pursuit of belonging comes from the safety of numbers. When a tiger attacks us, we want to have others around to help fend it off. We feel more secure when we know others will come to our aid in times of need.

Advocacy is all about providing support and encouragement for a cause. In the case of your friends, the cause is the relationship. Let your friends know that you are there for them in times of need. You can always be a shoulder to cry on or a hand to help lift them up. However, you should only make promises that you can keep. If Aragorn runs away at the first sign of danger, the promise of his sword means very little in the future. Here are a few ways you can be an advocate for your friend:

1. **Empathize.** Use your skills in attunement and communication to let your friends know that you understand how they feel. When you empathize with their situation, your friends feel less alone in their problems. Remember to use reflective phrases such as "it sounds like..." to help your friends feel heard and understood.

2. **Group up.** The only thing worse than being attacked by a tiger is being alone when the tiger attacks. Let your friends know that they do not have to face their problems alone and that you are on their side. You can be a significant resource for emotional support and security.

3. **Respond to requests for aid.** The beacons are lit! Your friends might also ask you for help, in which case you can rise to the occasion. When your friend is in dire need, do what you can to make those needs your priority. Life happens, which means that sometimes our friends might no longer have a place to work or a place to stay. All of us hope that others would come to our aid in those moments, and so we must be prepared to do the same.

Friendship Fortifier #4: Gifts

Gift-giving is by no means an essential part of friendship. However, gifts can be symbolic. When we send flowers to a loved one after they experience a death in the family, that gift is not intended to provide them with sustenance or financial security. Rather, many gifts are used to convey messages of love, pride, and empathy.

Some people are more able to receive those messages through gifts, rather than words. I might say "thank you for being my friend," but the words may not get the message across as well as a bag of candy or a new t-shirt.

Theoretically, this is because some of us pay more attention to certain messages of love and connection than others. A book called *The Five Love Languages: How to Express Heartfelt Commitment to Your Mate* claims that each of us has a primary "love language," or type of message that resonates most strongly with us in romantic relationships. These include gifts, spending time together, affirmation or compliments, acts of service or advocacy, and physical touch. Although we aren't (necessarily) trying to romance our friends, we do want them to know that they are loved. Here are a few ways to use gifts to fortify your friendships:

1. **Commemorate important dates.** Did you know that August 5th is Friendship Day in the United States? Gifts can be used to help highlight a specific date, such as a birthday or a friendship anniversary. Use these to communicate the importance of the relationship and demonstrate your remembrance of these events.

2. **Express pride or gratitude.** Gifts can be used as vehicles for other friendship fortifiers. You can show your friends how proud or thankful you are with even the simplest of gifts.

3. **The friendship totem.** Sometimes life takes our friends to other parts of the state, country, or even to the other side of the world. The distance makes it difficult to stay in touch and communicate feelings of love and connection. One way to ease the difficulty of long-distance friendship is to provide a friendship totem, or a gift that symbolizes your relationship. Psychologists call this the "transitional object," a sort of representation of the friendship that helps ease your parting. Give your friend something to help keep you in mind.

Friendship Fortifier #5: Forgiveness

I have a friend who is chronically late.

By default, whenever we plan to spend time together, I always expect a 15 to 30-minute delay before they arrive. Sometimes I will get a text message from them right at the time we were planning to meet up somewhere that says, "I just woke up, be there in 20." When they finally arrive, they always apologize and thank me for waiting.

I love my friend very much. One of his quirks is lateness, and I have come to accept this. However, I would argue that the relationship remains stable in part because of my willingness to forgive and my friend's willingness to ask for forgiveness.

All of us are guilty of making mistakes in relationships. Friendship follies happen unintentionally, and so we must find ways to make amends and ask forgiveness. Perhaps even more importantly, we must be willing to offer forgiveness for the sake of love.

When we forgive, we send the message that the relationship matters more to us than the temporary feelings of anger, sadness, or irritation. Learning to forgive takes time, and a degree of emotional regulation skill, to master. Let me give you a few ways to incorporate forgiveness into your friendships:

1. **Accept a few follies.** All of us are perfectly imperfect, after all. Some people are better at avoiding friendship follies than others, but that does not make them more or less worthy of your love. Recognize that you and your friends are going to make mistakes and be ready to respond with acts of forgiveness.

2. **Avoid retaliation.** Do your best not to lash out when your friends do stupid things. However, sometimes it can be helpful to let others know how you feel when those things happen. Your friends may not realize how irritated you feel when they eat the last slice of pizza or ignore your text messages. Find ways to calmly and privately communicate your needs so that your friends can understand how to adjust and improve.

3. **Notice your own mistakes.** When you think you have made a mistake, ask for forgiveness. It is typically better to apologize for something you thought was hurtful than to ignore wrongdoing.

Friendship Fortifier #6: Quality Time

Friendship takes time.

A lot of time, in fact.

Research published in the *Journal of Personal and Social Relationships* indicated that it takes over fifty hours of socializing to go from acquaintance to a casual friend. After that, it can take another forty hours to be considered an authentic friend. And, according to that research, close friendships take at least two-hundred hours together to form. I would argue that those hours must be quality hours of mutual engagement and not just time spent sitting in the same room together. If you spent that time working a job at minimum wage, close friendship is nearly a $2,000 investment.

Time is a resource. Many of us become so busy with our day-to-day lives that we are left with insufficient resources allocated to friendship.

If you hope to develop deep and meaningful friendships, you will need to clear some space in your calendar. Here are a few tips to make it easier:

1. **Choose weekends or weeknights.** If school or work keeps you busy during your week, you might need to get creative to block out time for friendship. One trick I recommend to clients is to focus on freeing up either their weekends or their weeknights. For example, if you dedicate one or two weeknights to friendship, you can use the weekend to recharge and catch up on other responsibilities.

2. **Coordinate sleep schedules.** One of my friends was a total night owl. They would stay up until three or four in the morning, sleep until noon, and repeat the cycle. As a morning person who often goes to bed around seven or eight, this made it difficult for us to spend time together. Sleep takes up about 1/3 of the day, and so

adjusting the time frame can make significant openings in the schedule. Find ways to compromise in the name of friendship so that sleep does not keep you from connection.

3. **Put your phone away.** Cell phones are awesome, but they distract us from spending quality time. When you are with your friends, do your best to make the most of the time you have together. Avoid letting outside distractions like phones interfere with the in-person connection.

Friendship Fortifier #7: Openness

When we are open with our friends, we invite them to understand our inner selves. We also tend to feel more drawn to the people that open up with us. However, finding the right degree of openness can be challenging. Remember the Walls of Emotional Distance and the Brambles of Bellyaching? When we are too open or too closed off, we keep people from feeling safe when they are with us.

Practice makes perfect when it comes to openness, and so you will want to find good opportunities for self-disclosure to happen in your relationships. You may want to open up about your intense fear of babies or your secret love for *My Little Pony*, but you may not want to engage in that sort of sharing while at school or work.

Here are a few ideas to help you find opportunities for openness:

1. **No need to rush.** Do not feel pressured to open up too quickly with others, and do not expect openness early on in the relationship. Remember, close friendship takes time. As the friendship develops, sharing will get easier.

2. **Establish trust.** Let your friends know that you are someone that can be trusted with vulnerability. Sometimes it can be helpful to offer "retroactive confidentiality," which means that you will keep anything they say confidential whenever they request it. Avoid sharing anything your friends tell you about themselves with others unless they explicitly give you permission to do. When in doubt, keep it private.

3. **Listen.** Your friends may be trying to open up to you in small ways all the time. Even small self-disclosures like their favorite foods or their feelings about a television show are ways your friend is trying to be open with you. Do not take small sharing for granted. Your friends want you to know them better just as much as you want them to know you.

Friendship Fortifiers #8 and #9: Teaching and Learning

"Will you teach me how to lift weights?"

This is the question that launched our very own Daniel Wendler on a journey of physical transformation. Dan knew that I was a college track coach, and he wanted me to help him improve his fitness levels. When we started out, Dan's poor flexibility and balance made tying his own shoes a challenge. Hundreds of workouts later, Dan blew my mind by deadlifting four-hundred pounds.

Although Dan learned some valuable lessons about strength training and made incredible physical gains, the time and focus of teaching him to lift provided us with a chance to become much closer as friends.

We are "swolemates" for life.

When we find things to teach our friends, we provide gifts of knowledge and receive opportunities to become closer as friends.

Conversely, our friends have a wealth of knowledge to share with us. When I began to develop my career as an author and public speaker, I relied heavily on Dan's wise teachings. And look! You are reading a book on friendship, largely in part because of things I learned from my friend.

Find ways to teach and learn from your friends, such as:

1. **Share your expertise.** If you have a particular skill or hobby, try bringing your friend into the fold. As the expert, you can share insider tips that will help your friends find early success and enjoyment. Sometimes it can be difficult for your friends to ask for you to teach them, and so you will want to find ways to offer

wisdom without making it feel demeaning. The best way to do this is to make it an invitation, rather than an order. For example, you might say "I love cooking brisket, if you ever want to learn a few of my cooking secrets let me know!" rather than "Let me teach you how to cook a brisket."

2. **Disclose a weakness.** If you know your friend is better than you at something, sometimes it can be helpful to point that out. Tell your musically-inclined friend that you are not so good at playing guitar, but that you would love any advice they could offer. Disclosing a weakness is also a way to provide a compliment or affirmation of your friend's skill, and so they will be pleased to hear you want to learn from them.

3. **Ask for feedback.** Everyone loves giving advice. When you ask your friends to evaluate your performance critically, you open yourself up to their teachings. Your friends will appreciate having an opportunity to share their thoughts and feelings about something you have done, and it can help set the tone for you to provide feedback to them in the future.

Friendship Fortifier #10: Discovery

As you and your friends master each other's skills and grow in the relationship, you will want to avoid the folly of stagnation. You could hypothetically teach each other everything you know, but eventually, you would run out of things to talk about.

Discover new hobbies, skills, and experiences together. The universe is filled with infinite knowledge and boundless opportunities for exploration and learning. However, you do not (necessarily) need to leave the atmosphere to find something new together.

Together, you could learn to dance or use martial arts, try a random restaurant, watch a new television series, or go on an adventure in the big city. These experiences create opportunities for shared memories, the backbone of emotional intimacy. As you discover the world together, you will discover more about each other.

Use these friendship fortifiers to provide a much-needed boost to your relationships. Your capacity for forgiveness and gratitude can affirm the spark of a new friendship just as much as it can bolster current connections. You have the power to breathe life into your friendships, and for that, I am proud of you.

Chapter Summary

Friendship fortifiers are skills you can use to strengthen and grow your relationships. Understanding the importance of time spent together, being supportive, and demonstrating pride for your friends can make a significant difference.

Questions to Ponder:

- Do any of these fortifiers come easier to you than others? Why or why not?

- Who in your life embodies or role-models fortifiers like gratitude and gift-giving? What makes them so good at those skills?

- Do any of your relationships need a boost? How can you reach out to them?

CHAPTER 11
REACH OUT

I haven't always been good at friendship. In fact, most of my life was spent in an introvert's paradise, pouring hours into video games, reading fantasy or sci-fi novels, or training for sports. If my lovely wife (and high school sweetheart) hadn't pursued me as diligently as she did, I would have continued to progress into adulthood without anyone I could trust or be vulnerable with.

All of that changed when I bumped into Dan.

Dan and I attended graduate school together at the George Fox University Graduate School of Clinical Psychology. When we first met, I was dumbfounded. How could someone so humble and kind be a published author, a TEDx speaker, and as brilliant as he is - without being a total jerk?

I was fascinated.

So, I did something a bit outside of my comfort zone. I asked him out to lunch.

It was a new burger joint that had opened up near campus. The place was booming, and the orders were taking forever. As we ran out of small talk, I realized how crappy I was at making friends. It wasn't a business meeting, it wasn't a date, and so I had no idea what to do next. Thankfully we were both in training to become psychologists, and so I went for vulnerability. "Dan, I really suck at this. I haven't made a genuine friend (not counting my wife) since probably fourth grade. I think you are cool, and I kind of want to try being friends." Dan grinned, breathed a sigh of relief, and said: "Thank goodness, I was starting to worry you didn't like me."

Lunch turned into late night Dungeons and Dragons games, being workout buddies at the campus weight room, and stressing about school and life together. Some of my fondest memories in grad school involve processing emotional struggles together while doing bench press. In fact, our mantra for workout sessions was "in the gym we lift many heavy things, and some of those things are weights." We share a profound connection, and I thank God every day for bringing Dan into my life.

Later in our friendship journey, Dan and I realized just how badly we needed each other. Both of us lacked meaningful connection outside of the family unit. Both of us needed peers to talk to about life and career stress. Both of us yearned for someone to appreciate the sweet joy of eating socially inappropriate amounts of gum. And neither of us thought the other needed connection.

If you gain nothing else from this book, I hope you remember this:

Reach out.

Someone needs your friendship.

A study from 2017 published in the *American Psychologist* showed us that social disconnection is becoming a major public health crisis at the level of obesity, smoking, air pollution, and alcohol abuse.

If you knew that your friendship could cure diseases like cancer, I bet my mustache that we would find you sprinting through hospitals all over the world, giving hugs and loving words to everyone you met.

Your friendship can save lives.

Look for those who need a boost, a kind word, a warm smile. Look for those who smile bravely and say "I am fine" when their hearts cry out for connection. Look for those who sit alone and offer them a place at your table.

Every soul is worthy of belonging.

Rejoice in the perfect imperfection of human brokenness. Find ways to look past your biases, your wounds, and embrace the overlooked and forgotten.

You are not forsaken, you are my friend.

Do not scoff at the hands outstretched on your behalf. Just as you reach out to others, let others reach out to you.

And together, we can make this lonely planet a little less so.

PART 3
LOOKING IN BETWEEN

My first school dance went about as well as you might expect.

Our teachers had given us some basic partner dancing instructions, just enough to do the middle school shuffle, and despite our protest and screams of terror, we were shoved out onto the dance floor.

The DJ cued up the first slow song and, not unlike a collar-popped and rainbow vest clad Moses, split the sea of boys to one side and girls to the other.

And then, he raised his mic and announced that "Mrs. Bartlett is offering extra credit to anyone who dances with a partner for this dance! Whoooooo's feeling it? Aw YEAH! Slow dance, baby!"

How *dare* she?

I was certainly afraid of dancing, but even more afraid of not getting a good grade from Mrs. Bartlett.

As my very soul split in twain, a scene from *The Lord of the Rings: Return of the King* came to me. You know, the one where Aragorn and the army of men stand at the gates of Mordor to distract the eye of Sauron. Despite facing certain disfigurement and death, Aragorn raises his blade and charges the enemy horde.

And so, I crossed the vast gender expanse and asked one of the girls to dance.

I didn't realize at the time that that was the easy part.

My gracious partner and I went arm in arm, hand in hand. And that's when I blew it.

In my mind, we were going to do the dance in *Beauty and the Beast*, which meant I needed to move dramatically and guide my partner in a theatrical sweeping waltz. There were three problems with this tactic. One, I had never danced with a partner before. Two, I had no clue how to dance like that. And three, I gave my partner exactly no warning of what I was about to do.

Thankfully, no one got injured. At least not physically.

You see, relationships are a lot like dancing. As long as both partners communicate and move together in unison, the dance is an enjoyable shared experience.

Sadly, most of us are terrible at the relationship dance. This is particularly true when it comes to friendship. As you have learned from previous chapters, friendship is complex. Each partner comes with their own set of beliefs, needs, and attachment styles that guide their approach to the friendship dance.

You have learned a great deal about looking within yourself and making changes to become a better friend and a healthier human being. You have also learned how to bring these insights into relationships and extend the hand of friendship to others. Now, here in Part 3, you will learn the dance of friendship.

CHAPTER 12
THE ART OF THE AUCTIONEER

Second only to the homecoming football game, the country fair was the biggest thing in town for the small municipality of Cottonwood, Idaho, population 800 humans and 1600 cattle.

If you have never been to a county fair, think of it as a cross between a talent show and a carnival, where everyone in town brings in their prized crops, baked goods, and livestock to sell to the highest bidder. This is why auctions are the centerpiece of most fairs.

The dusty air was always thick with the smell of animal poop, cotton candy, and sweaty farmers. Ah, the memories. Eager buyers would crowd into a showman arena where sellers would bring out the cows, sheep, pigs, and other livestock for sale. And then, a person called the auctioneer would start rapid-fire shouting sale numbers. To the untrained ear, auctioneers sound a bit like redneck beatboxers. In the span of just about two seconds, an auctioneer can spit out "Alright, let's start bidding at $100, $110, $150, $200..." as they increase the number based on the highest bid.

The buyers would indicate that they were willing to take the last shouted number by raising a hand or waving at the auctioneer. The auctioneer would say "And we've got $200! Do we have $250? $250 anyone? $225?" If no one raised their hand to raise the bid, the final bidder gets the purchase. Or, sometimes the competing bidder will shake their head to indicate that they have reached their limit. "$200 going once, going twice, SOLD!"

Things are different in the great county fair of friendship, but not much.

Rather than bid on possessions, people make bids for interpersonal connection. Connection helps us to feel understood and valued, which makes it easier to have our needs met. If we are hungry and all out of food, we want others to understand our feelings so that they can help us find a good meal or comfort us. As relationally-wired beings, we crave the connection that is offered through relationships. And so, connection is a hot bidding item in the great interpersonal auction.

Unlike raising a hand in an auction, a bid for connection can appear many different ways. Friends ask us for our thoughts and feelings. Coworkers ask us out to lunch. Cashiers ask us how our day is going. People in elevators make jokes about it being Monday to try and lighten the mood, and not just because Mondays are the worst, but also because they are looking for human connection and understanding. Many bids for connection are subtle, which is why we tend to miss them when they happen.

Isn't it amazing how auctioneers are able to speak so quickly and also watch for bids in a massive crowd of country folk?

The art of the auctioneer is the key to finding new friends and deepening current friendships. We must learn to watch for and notice bids for connection amidst the bustle of everyday living.

So, how do we do that?

Use the skills you have developed in communication and attunement. Remember, this is all about sending and receiving interpersonal messages. The first step in noticing a bid for connection requires being able to identify it as an attempt to connect, rather than an attempt to create distance or harm. Next, you must learn how to respond to bids in a way that is congruent with your values. Finally, you can observe their reaction to understand whether or not you are both on the same page.

Identifying the Bid

Imagine what auctions would look like if the auctioneers were unable to identify bids from the crowd. The auctioneer might think that every sneeze, fart, and head nod was a bid, in which case all chaos would break loose. Or, they would miss every bid and assume no one is interested in buying.

This is why it is so important to identify interpersonal bids for connection accurately.

Traditional psychoanalyst and psychological theorist Dr. Karen Horney proposed that interpersonally, people tend to use behaviors from three main categories: **moving toward, moving away,** and **moving against.** I would also add a fourth category, which I will call **moving stuff.** Each of these behaviors can be bids for connection in some way, and so we will dive into each of these individually. As you read through each category, try to think of examples from your life when you have noticed these in the past. When you are able to notice these behaviors in others accurately, you will master the art of the auctioneer.

Moving Toward

When we are interested in something, we tend to move in closer. For example, if you notice a $20 bill on the ground, you might move closer to inspect it. Similarly, behaviors that are moving toward tend to be interpersonal messages of interest, whether by asking about your day or bringing you a cookie. They are attempts made by the other person to indicate some motivation to interact with you or develop a deeper relationship.

Behaviors that can be categorized as moving toward tend to fall on a spectrum of intimacy. In its purest form, moving toward is an overt expression of desire for connection. Loved ones will often use moving toward bids to explicitly indicate a desire for having their attachment needs met. For some, this might be something physical, such as a hug or giving a gift, or verbal, such as asking to spend time with you. For others, this might look like giving help or assistance, such as offering to help mow your lawn or give you a ride somewhere. These sorts of bids for connection tend to be the easiest to identify. However, the less intimate bids for connection are more challenging to notice. It may be as subtle as a friendly smile, holding open a door for you, saving you a seat in class, or trying to make you laugh with a pun.

Moving Away

When we want to create distance with something, we move away. If you noticed a giant venomous snake on the ground, for example, you might want to get out of there. People often use moving away behaviors to express disinterest, discomfort, or a desire to find safety. This may look like ending a conversation prematurely, turning away to face someone else, or leaving the room entirely.

Although it may not seem like it, sometimes when people engage in moving away behaviors, they are actually trying to bid for connection. For example, if you got into a fight with your sibling they might hide in their room until you come talk to them. Similarly, sometimes people become quiet when they are upset. These sorts of reactions may indicate that the other person wants you to console them or make amends, which is a bid for connection with you. However, more often than not these signals are used to tell you that the other person is not looking for further interaction or relationship.

Moving Against

When we feel threatened or when we want to confront something, we move against it. If you saw a nasty cockroach on the floor, you might try to squish it or scare it outside. People use moving against behaviors to communicate anger, feelings of injustice, or assert control or dominance. Your boss may yell at you because you made a mistake on the job. Someone at the grocery store may get upset if they think you are cutting in line. Your friend might punch you in the shoulder after you said something insensitive. These actions are intended to send you the message that something is wrong, something is unsafe, and that something needs to be done about it.

These same moving against behaviors can also be used to bid for connection. For example, your friend might grump at you for taking the last piece of pizza. If your friend has special dietary restrictions and you eat the last slice of gluten-free, they may be trying to get you to understand that your ignorance made them feel hurt and undervalued. These bids are particularly important to notice when we want to make amends or repair the relationship. When we fail to identify or address them, moving against and moving away signals can lead to loss of relationship. Never fear, we will talk more about making repairs in the next chapter.

Moving Stuff

Sometimes, interpersonal messages are purely transactional. If you are not tall enough to reach something on the top shelf, you might ask someone tall or ladder-equipped for help. Behaviors that are categorized as moving stuff may also have flavors of moving towards or moving against, but the primary message is about accomplishing a task. People may ask us to hold the elevator door for them or pass the salt without having any sort of clear motivation for connection.

We tend to over-interpret these sorts of behaviors as having deeper meaning. Just because someone asks to borrow your pencil does not mean you are destined to be together forever. However, if they ask for your pencil as a way to break the ice and start a conversation, they may be looking for connection. And maybe you will be together forever, who knows?

Nearly every interpersonal behavior or message can be lumped into one of these four categories. As you learn to identify what messages people send, you will get better at recognizing bids for connection. However, people are complex. You might be able to categorize the behavior as moving towards or against, but not everyone is good at sending the right messages. Sometimes you will be tasked with interpreting their true intent.

Interpreting the Bid

You have taken the first step by noticing interpersonal messages. If you struggle with noticing social cues, that may have been the most challenging step. Now you are ready to learn how to decode those messages.

This just in: aliens have just landed on planet Earth. They look like bear-sized armadillos, and they speak mostly gibberish. Thankfully, the aliens seem to be trying to communicate with us rather than eat our brains or enslave our children. For reasons unknown, NASA has assigned you the task of learning to understand them.

For some of us, this job would seem easier than trying to understand other humans.

As a translator of bids for connection, you can use the same techniques you might try when interpreting alien communication. Unlike in the movie *Arrival*, this will not require programming an advanced computer to identify ink-spray patterns. At least, it shouldn't. Instead, you can use context to get a rough idea of what the other person is trying to communicate.

The term "context" refers to the surrounding information that is used to interpret the meaning of a word. Words can mean different things based on the context, which is why "You look funny" means something very different from "You are funny" and "You smell funny."

When we think of context, we typically focus on the content of what is said to understand the meaning. This is important, but it doesn't capture the full picture. For example, someone might say something like "You are terrible." If we only try to understand the context of what was said, we might interpret that the other person is trying to insult or embarrass us. However, if we notice that they are smiling and shaking their head, we might interpret their meaning to be more of a friendly tease. Or, if this same message was said by a prosecuting attorney in the courtroom, you might interpret that as an accusation.

People send verbal and non-verbal messages to each other constantly. Although the content of the message tends to be clear, the meaning of the content is up for interpretation. Sometimes people say one thing but mean something else entirely. Or, they might say one thing but mean multiple things at once.

By using context cues, we can make an educated guess as to what the other person truly means.

Here are **three main context clues** you want to look for when identifying bids for connection:

Clue #1: Setting

The setting includes *who, what,* and *where* the interaction happens. If social interaction was a Broadway performance, the setting would be the storyline, the backdrop, and the characters on stage. We might be able to guess what will happen in the next scene based on the scene before. A scene that features a hero and a villain is likely to look different from a scene between two star-crossed lovers. Furthermore, a scene that has a fiery backdrop might feel different from one held in a majestic fairy garden.

Think about how *who* you are interacting with can affect the way you would interpret their behavior. If someone were to ask you out to lunch, this would feel differently coming from a friend rather than your boss. Similarly, *what* is happening in the interaction can also affect the meaning. You might feel differently if boss asks you out to lunch right after you messed up on a project, rather than during a friendly conversation. *Where* the interaction takes place is also important, as the message may be altered to fit the situation. A hug at a funeral means something different than a hug after winning the state championship.

If you pay attention to who, what, and where the interaction is happening, you will find it much easier to intuit the meaning of their message.

Clue #2: Emotional Tone

The tone of the message can clue you into the emotional experience of the other person. This is important to catch, as it can also help you recognize whether the person is moving towards, against, or away from you emotionally.

For example, when someone says, "your hair looks great," the emotional expression that accompanies the message can drastically affect the meaning of their words. If their voice indicates sincerity and warmth, they may be giving you a compliment. If their voice sounds sarcastic, it was probably an insult.

Many of us are able to pick up the emotional tone of spoken language. Some people, particularly younger Autistic folks, may have a more difficult time picking up on emotional tone. One helpful workaround is to imagine that there was some sort of thematic background music playing at the time, like in the movies. If you can imagine intense battle music, the person is probably angry. If a solemn violin solo is a better fit, they might be feeling down or sad.

Clue #3: Body Language

Learning to read body language is critical for interpreting bids for connection. We tend to more freely communicate our inner experiences non-verbally, which means that we can use body language to gauge what the other person is thinking or feeling.

For example, let's imagine that we are coworkers, and you have just asked me how my day is going. I might respond verbally by saying "It's going well, thanks," and my tone might sound fairly positive, but my arms are crossed, my eyes are red and puffy, and my lip is quivering. You could probably guess that my day is not going well, after all.

Worry not, dear reader, my day really is going quite well.

Pay attention to the signals that people send with their bodies. Look for signs of emotion through facial expressions and posture. When I said, "It's going well, thanks," I was also communicating that I was feeling sad and distressed. As you learn to integrate the content with the context clue of body language, you will begin to notice extra messages being sent your way.

Respond to the Bid

You have noticed the message being sent your way, and you have interpreted the meaning based on context clues. Now comes the moment where you need to respond. This can be a problem for many of

us, as there are infinite ways of responding in any given social interaction.

Sometimes the other person's behavior indicates some distancing or
disinterest in further interaction, and that is okay. Your responses
will also depend on your needs and values. If you are not looking for
friendship, but someone sends you a bid for connection, you may
not feel motivated to respond with warmth or interest.

And yet, here you sit, reading a book on friendship. My guess is that
when bids for connection come your way, you will want to know
how to respond in turn.

When I do not know what to say or how to react to certain messages,
I fall back on what I call the **ERA** of communication: **Emote, Reflect,**
and **Add**. Let me break these down.

Emote

The easiest way to respond to any message is to emote or display
some form of emotion. If someone tells you a long story about
their weekend, and you are unsure of how to respond to what they
said, you can always just nod and smile. Just make sure the emotion
matches the content of what they just shared. If they told you that
their cat just died, do not smile. I repeat, do not smile when they tell
you their cat just died. Instead, you might nod understandingly and
show sadness using your eyes and mouth. Emoting is a simple way
you can show that you were paying attention and you understood
the emotional content of what was shared.

Reflect

Emoting will only take you so far. Eventually, you are going to have
to use your words. Reflecting is a technique that therapists use to
help their clients feel heard and understood. You can reflect what
someone says to you by restating something they said, or you can try
to guess the way they are feeling based on the context clues. You can
start off a reflection by saying "It sounds like you…" or "It seems like
you…" statements. For example, if I just finished telling you about

my new job you could reflect by saying "It sounds like you are excited about your new job!"

Add

No matter how good you are at reflecting, unless you contribute something new to the conversation it will make your partner feel like they are talking to a parrot. "I had a terrible weekend." "It sounds like you had a terrible weekend." "Yes... it was bad." "It seems like you felt it was bad." Although these sorts of interactions might show the other person that you were listening, they do not do much for moving the conversation forward.

When you are able to add your experiences and ideas to the interaction, you give the other person the chance to understand you better. Sometimes you can share your emotional reaction to what they just said or did by using "that made me feel..." and "I am starting to feel..." statements. Or, perhaps something that was said has sparked a new thought or idea that you want to share, in which case you can use "that made me think of..." and "I just thought of..." statements. You can also add a question at the end to keep the conversation going.

The richest responses tend to combine all three: demonstrate your experience through body language, reflect what they said, and then add some of your own thoughts or feelings. If we are having a conversation about the arcade, you might smile and laugh, say "Wow! It sounds like you had a lot of fun! That made me think of how long it has been since I've gone to the arcade. We should go sometime, what do you think?"

Read the Reaction

You are doing great! You have noticed the message, interpreted the message, and responded, but your task is not complete. Now you must watch to see how your response was received because their reaction will give you another message about the interaction. From there, you can go back to the same steps as you used at the beginning: notice, interpret, respond, and read.

Hopefully, the other person has reacted in the way that you expected. If they said they were hungry, and you responded by offering them a sandwich, you would hope that they would react by saying "thank you" and accepting your offering. If they have offered an invitation to a party this weekend, you would hope that they seem excited when you accept.

Unfortunately, people do not always react in predictable or kind ways. Sometimes we say or do things that unintentionally trigger uncomfortable feelings of anger, fear, or disgust in others. We might misinterpret someone's behavior as being a bid for friendship and closeness, only to be met with rejection. We cannot control how people will react. However, we can always try to make amends.

As you learn how to identify bids for connection and respond to them well, you will notice opportunities for friendship all around you. You may notice bids that were previously ignored, such as when the guy next door offers to watch your puppy next time you travel somewhere. You may notice these bids happening in your current relationships, which will allow you to help the people in your life feel understood and supported by you. Our lives get us so wrapped up in school and work that we often miss the things that are most important to us. If you value friendship and you hope to find deeper connection, learn to master the art of the auctioneer.

Chapter Summary

The art of the auctioneer is all about learning to notice and respond to the bids for connection that people send our way. As a species that is hardwired for relationship, we are driven to find belonging and connect with one another. You have the ability to pick up on bids for connection from others by noticing their behavior, interpreting their meaning, and responding in a way that lets them feel understood and seen by you.

Questions to Ponder:

- Do you know of anyone who has been sending you bids for connection? What is that like for you?

- What ways have you responded to bids in the past?

- How have the experiences in your life affected your awareness to bids for connection?

CHAPTER 13
RUPTURE AND REPAIR

A few years ago, I was lifting weights at a local university weight room. I was distracted during my workout by a strangely dressed young man. He wore a bright yellow bandana and one of those old-school bodybuilder tank tops, and his facial expression indicated that he meant business. He puffed out his chest and slapped his hands against his legs and core to get himself pumped up. And then, he began loading a substantial amount of weight on a barbell.

As a former college athlete and coach, I know a thing or two about weightlifting. I typically do not give advice in the weight room (unless asked), but I think it is always a good idea to warm up before trying to lift heavy things. When I told him this, he returned my advice with a scowl and an unrelenting stare as he stomped up to the bar to deadlift the weight and yelled, "THIS IS WHAT I DO!"

Although the bar did not move, his yell was impressive. And so was the smell. And so was his face as he awkwardly waddled out to change his shorts.

When I wrote this book, my fear was that I would be like tank top guy – bellowing loudly while producing nothing but crap. But over the years, I have learned that I actually *can* do a few things, and I hope to share those things with others.

For example, did you know that when you lift weights, you are actually causing tiny tears in your muscle tissue?

Your body is literally getting ripped.

These tears are important. As your muscle tissues break down, your body adapts through a process of repair that ultimately strengthens the area and prepares it for the future.

You must activate and stress your muscles in order to make them grow, otherwise your body begins to weaken and atrophy. Similarly, human relationships require regular engagement in order to grow stronger. Over time, our friendships grow stronger as we learn to trust and love more powerfully than before.

And yet, as we learn to lift each other up we also risk more serious relational injuries. Even the most careful professional powerlifters pull muscles and tear tendons.

We get into arguments with one another. We say hurtful things. We forget birthdays and anniversaries, and we miss or ignore bids for connection. These relational injuries, known by psychologists as "ruptures," are the result of attachment needs being unmet. All of us desire safety and belonging in our relationships. When something happens that indicates separation or rupture, we experience intense suffering.

When our bodies are injured, we naturally seek ways to soothe the pain and heal. An ice pack always feels good on a sprained ankle, and a bandage helps the papercut sting a bit less. Over time, these efforts help the body to repair and regain functioning.

When our relationships are injured, however, we do not always pursue such repair. Disagreements lead to blocking one another on Facebook. Hurtful words catalyze the flames of conflict until the friendship is reduced to ash.

Rupture is a normal part of every friendship. If both parties are trying to be open and trusting in the relationship, they are opening themselves up in a vulnerable way. As we know, vulnerability is a risk that requires courage. Just as the athlete continues to train in the pursuit of their goals, we who seek friendships with meaning and significance are happy to take that risk

Now that you are becoming somewhat of a friendship expert, you are ready to learn how to recognize and repair relational ruptures.

How to Recognize Ruptures

When I was a young warthog, I loved making water balloons.

I would get the party-sized balloons and fill them up with a garden hose until they were the size of watermelons. My siblings and I would gather around the super balloons and poke them until they would pop, and typically one or two of us would get totally soaked.

Water balloon ruptures are similar to relational ruptures. The shared enjoyment of the balloon, mixed with the occasional poke or prod to test the tenacity of the rubber, represents the fun of friendship. However, some poking and prodding leads to strong tension, a small leak, and a burst of icy water. Some of us react strongly to the rupture, with screams of fear and shock. Others might create distance and run away from the blast. When these things happen in our relationships, we must understand the cause, the reaction, and the aftermath in order to make amends.

Imagine that you and a friend are out for a walk together. You are enjoying the sunshine, smelling the fresh air, and watching the squirrels tempt fate by sprinting back and forth across the roadway.

The two of you are having a friendly conversation about the latest in national news, when suddenly, your friend becomes tearful. You, being an excellent person and a friendship expert, ask them what is wrong. Your friend continues to cry, shakes their head, and begins walking in the opposite direction.

What just happened?

Each of us has experienced moments of confusion, anger, and frustration in our friendships. When our relationships rupture, we often feel at a loss for how to respond. And often, we are left asking ourselves "what just happened?" in a sort of relational autopsy. Unlike with an actual autopsy, your relationship is probably not dead. There will always be ways for you to seek repair and revive the relationship. But first, you have to recognize when the rupture happens.

Relational ruptures are easy to recognize when you can identify three main factors: the cause, the reaction, and the aftermath.

First, we have to notice the cause of the rupture. Was an attachment need unmet? Did someone miss a bid for connection? Was there some miscommunication or mistake? Next, understanding the severity of the reaction will help us recognize how much stress the rupture has caused. Finally, we must flesh out where the rupture has taken place. Is this because of my unmet needs, or theirs? Which of us seems more hurt or wounded? Your ability to understand these factors can dramatically affect the potential for repair.

The Cause

The most important thing to remember is that the rupture can only happen when there is a relationship. This means that both parties are somehow involved in whatever causes it. We typically notice the cause when others say or do things that cause us stress or pain. I felt angry when my friend made a sexist comment. You felt worried when your friend said she was moving across the country.

However, when our actions create the rupture, we sometimes miss it. This is because the cause tends to be more subtle than the consequence. In other words, you might not notice when you said something insensitive to your friend, but you would surely notice when they became tearful and walked away.

Ruptures can be caused by just about anything. However, people tend to feel the most wounded when one of these things happen:

1. **Insensitivity and ignorance.** When we are not attuned to the needs of our friends, we sometimes say or do things that cause them hurt. For example, if I forget that my friend identifies as gender-fluid and I call them by the wrong pronoun, my insensitivity to their needs may cause them to feel unwanted or unimportant in the relationship. Or, if my friend invites me to spend time with them on the weekend and I turn them down without giving a reason, I may have been insensitive to a bid for connection. If I ignore their reactions of confusion or hurt, intentionally or otherwise, I communicate that my needs are greater than theirs.

2. **Disagreement and disrespect.** Nine out of ten scientists agree, friendship requires two or more people. We don't really count the tenth scientist, though, since she has two heads and is best friends with herself. As relationships are defined by the meeting of two distinct souls with unique opinions and beliefs, disagreement is bound to happen. Some of us are able to handle that sort of conflict, agree to disagree, and appreciate the diversity in the relationship. However, many of us are guilty of seeing our own views as being better or superior. When we assume that our perspective is the right one, we communicate disrespect for anything different.

3. **Betrayal of trust.** We share intimate secrets with our friends to help them understand our innermost selves. Vulnerability is a risk. When trusted information is shared without permission, the risk of harm is great. Similarly, when promises are broken or we are taken advantage of, the relationship is cheapened or made to seem meaningless. Ruptures caused by betrayals of trust tend to be the most severe and difficult to repair.

Anyone who has experienced these things knows the pain that comes with rupture. Although we hope to avoid being insensitive or accidentally spilling each other's secrets, each of us is flawed and prone to making mistakes. However, by being aware of the potential causes of rupture, we can more readily address it when it happens.

The Reaction

The most severe reactions to rupture are the easiest to identify. When our friends blow up and scream at us, we tend to notice. However, more subtle reactions often go unnoticed. Over time, the unnoticed lower severity ruptures can culminate in a resounding relational eruption.

Noticing the signs of a mild to moderate rupture is essential for addressing relational issues early in their course. Everyone reacts to the cause of a rupture differently, so think of these more as guidelines than rules. Here are a few common reactions to causes of rupture.

1. **Distance and disengagement.** When confronted with danger, people tend to react with the fight, flight, or freeze response. A rupture that causes friends to stop talking or leave the room suddenly are examples of flight or freeze. This reaction indicates that something has disrupted the safety of the relationship. Where thoughts and feelings were once freely shared, now those seem unsafe to let out. People who are more like the Tortoise in their attachment may be prone to this reaction when a rupture occurs.

2. **Anger and retaliation.** These reactions are very easy to notice and can feel very threatening. Just like flight or freeze, the fight response is a powerful reaction to a lack of safety or threat of danger. A rupture that causes friends to start arguing or tossing insults suddenly is an example of the fight response. People who are more like the Hen or the Cat in their attachment may be prone to these kinds of reactions.

3. **Confusion and questioning.** Sometimes we will react to conflict by intellectualizing or problem-solving. This is a more sophisticated version of anger and retaliation, which is why we typically see it with adults. Rather than disengaging or arguing, some of us will react to ruptures by focusing on what happened and what was said rather than the feelings that were hurt. People who tend to rely on the Towers of Intellectualization may be more likely to do this than others.

Notice how our defenses and attachment styles can feed into the re-action. This is why it is so important to understand yourself, that way you are aware of how certain causes trigger your reactions. As rupture requires a relationship, you must now identify how each person has been affected.

The Aftermath

Some water balloon eruptions led to one of us taking more water than others, although it was rare for anyone to stay dry.

Now that you have a sense of the cause and effect of rupture, you can begin to think about how the rupture has affected both parties. This part is easier said than done, so I will give you a shortcut.

Ask yourself two questions:

1. *"Is this my stuff, or their stuff?"*

In other words, ask yourself if the rupture is happening because of your attachment needs and your defenses, or those of your friends. As you develop a greater sense of your contribution to the rupture, you will be more readily able to engage in repair.

1. *"Who seems more hurt by this?"*

Try to identify who has taken most of the water from the balloon. There might have been hurt on both sides, but chances are one person will seem more distressed by what happened.

How to Repair a Rupture

Unlike repairing a popped water balloon, relational repair is very possible.

There are four important steps for friends to follow as they work through relational ruptures.

First, the friendship must come to an understanding that a rupture has occurred by naming it. This provides a foundational agreement that something is off in the relationship that needs to be addressed. Second, each person must take turns attempting to describe their experiences of what happened. This allows both parties an opportunity to be vulnerable and provide insight to the other. Third, the friendship must take action to make amends and reconcile the rupture. And fourth, the friendship must problem-solve ways to meet each other's needs best and facilitate future communication. Let's break it down.

Name the Rupture

When I say "name" the rupture, what I mean is to point out that the rupture has happened clearly. I don't mean name it, as in "let's call this rupture George;" although, that could be fun.

Pause for a moment and identify the cause, the reaction, and the aftermath. Now, try to name what happened. Naming requires three parts: the cause, your emotional reaction, and an invitation to talk about it.

Focus on using phrases that start with "I feel like..." or "It seems like..." to help you communicate your understanding of the rupture. For example, you might say "I feel like what I said was hurtful in some way." This acknowledges that something you said might have caused a rupture and provides an opening for the other person to respond. Also, by phrasing it in a way that does not sound accusatory, your friend will be more likely to engage in the conversation and be vulnerable with you.

If your friend's words or actions seemed to cause the rupture, try saying "when you ... I felt [emotion words]." For example, you could try saying, "When you made that comment about *Twilight*, I felt sad and a bit hurt." This formula allows you to point out what you believe happened clearly and helps your friend understand how it made you feel.

Finally, always finish your naming by inviting the conversation to occur. "Can we talk about it?" "Would it be okay if we talked about what happened?" If your friend does not want to talk about it, you might need to give it some time. For example, people who have more of a Tortoise style of attachment may be tempted to withdraw until their emotions feel safer to share.

Here are a few other examples of how you can name the rupture:

- "I noticed that you weren't able to make it to my birthday party. When you weren't there, I felt very sad. Would it be okay if we talked about it?"

- "It seems like my comment about *Star Wars* being better than *Star Trek* made you upset. Can we talk about that?"

- "I am sorry for bringing up that embarrassing thing you did at the Christmas party, it seems like I made you angry and I am sorry. Do you mind if we talk about that for a minute?"

Describe the Reaction

Next, take turns describing your reactions to the rupture and share your perspectives. Think of this as a game of catch, where you and your friend take turns tossing some of your thoughts and feelings to one another.

You can continue to use phrases such as "I feel like..." and "it seems like..." to help you describe the reactions you observed. You can also try to guess what your friend's experience was by using phrases like "I wonder if what I said (or did) made you [emotion words]." For example, you might say "I wonder if when I ate the last piece of pizza, that made you feel angry." Be curious, and prioritize the relationship.

Give your friends time to share, and listen closely to their perspective. Each time you share with one another, the friendship develops insight. You learn what things are particularly hurtful to your friend. Your friend realizes what you are trying to communicate when you get quiet. This mutual understanding is a rich opportunity for the friendship to deepen in emotional intimacy and trust.

Reconcile the Rupture

Now that you have a sense of how the rupture affected the friendship, you are ready to take action to make amends. In keeping with the water balloon metaphor, this is the part where you give someone a towel and say "sorry."

Admitting wrongdoing takes courage. When you or your friend apologize for what happened, you are communicating with one another that you care more about the friendship than personal pride.

If appropriate, express an apology for any contribution you might have had in causing the rupture. Be authentic, and avoid sarcasm or passive aggression. For example, if you say "Oh, I am so sorry for making you freak out like a sissy when I said that thing about Jar Jar Binks" or "I feel kind of sorry for teasing you, but I was just trying to be funny," you will minimize their experience of hurt and ruin the apology altogether.

Explore Solutions

Now that amends have been made, you are ready to team up to find some solutions. You and your friend must now objectively look at the problem, side-by-side, to come up with ideas that will keep it from happening in the future.

Your solutions will depend on the situation and the needs of the friendship, so rather than giving you solutions I will suggest some things to avoid.

- **Do not begin to problem-solve until amends are fully made.** Make sure that you and your friend feel good about the resolution so that you have clear minds for finding solutions together.

- **Do not make promises that cannot be kept.** If you promise that you will never tease your friend again, even the most polite and wholesome tease may be interpreted as a breach of that promise.

- **Do not disrespect each other's ideas.** You just repaired a rupture, so the last thing you want to do is create another one. Be open, curious, and non-judgmental.

- **Do not forget to celebrate repair.** The friendship has survived! Take some time to notice and possibly celebrate your teamwork.

Rupture and repair are natural parts of the relational process. We are bound to make mistakes and step on each other's toes in the great dance of friendship. Rather than end the dance and say goodbye forever, slow down and take time to improve your footwork together.

Chapter Summary

Any relationship that means anything will have conflict. We say and do stupid things because we are human. Despite being wired for interconnectivity, we tend to misunderstand and offend one another. Learning how to make repairs when our relationships rupture is an essential skill for anyone who seeks to be a good friend. As you engage in relationships, pay attention to moments of misunderstanding and hurt, open channels of mutual communication, and collaborate together to find solutions.

Questions to Ponder:

- Have you experienced any major relational ruptures? What happened? How was it addressed?

- Looking back, have you caused any ruptures that need repair? Even old wounds need healing.

CHAPTER 14
THE POWER IMBALANCE

They say that if you weren't bullied growing up, you were probably the bully.

I disagree.

I believe that people can be both. I know that people can be both.

When I was in 5th grade, I went to a high school football game with my dad. He and some of his friends joined the rest of the crowd in the bleachers, while I went off to join the herd of kids playing catch and watching the game in the field nearby. I wasn't that interested in watching the game. The crisp autumn night was perfect for running around and having fun.

After a few hours of playing tag, one of the older kids said we should head over to the practice field to play some "real football." Most of the kids followed, and so I did too. The game was incredibly rough. People were tackling each other at full speed, with no protective equipment, causing bloody noses and plenty of bruises. One by one, most of the kids my age left and drifted back to watch the game. But I was tough, and I wanted to prove it.

I lined up once again with the other kids. Most of them were teenagers. My team was on defense. On a lucky play, I broke through their offense and tackled their quarterback. As I rose to my feet with a proud grin on my face, one of the guys on the other team grabbed me by my shirt and threw me on the ground.

"You think that was cool, you worthless turd?"

My smile went away. I shakily got up, dazed and afraid. "I was just trying to play."

"What, are you going to cry?" the shirt-grabber cackled as stepped up and stared me down with a malicious grin.

My mind raced, my heart panicked, and my eyes responded with tears.

"Shut up," laughed the quarterback, "you are actually crying. No way, he barely touched you."

He then swung a fist deep into my gut, "Now THAT is something worth crying over."

They laughed as one of them shoved me to the ground, and they left me there in the dirt.

That terrible night changed me. I never talked about what happened to anyone, and I made a promise that I would never be so vulnerable again.

I became obsessed with physical strength. I asked my dad to teach me how to lift weights and get stronger so that I could play college football. I began powerlifting at age ten and ate like a horse. My body responded in turn, and I quickly became one of the strongest athletes in the state. Weightlifting became my identity, and I was all too happy to share my latest feats.

Fast forward to my senior year of high school. I was a top recruit at some of the most prestigious schools in the nation for my athleticism, and I had earned it. I would spend hours outside of practice in the gym, lifting and slamming protein shakes. The first time I squatted over six-hundred pounds, I felt invincible.

I was standing in the football locker room after practice. One of my teammates, we'll call him Brian, had a habit of being a bit socially inappropriate. I thought Brian was just odd, but actually he was diagnosed with Asperger's and had trouble reading social cues. His locker was right next to mine. After practice one day, he began asking me a string of questions about the colleges that were recruiting me.

"Are you going to sign with Duke?"

"How many pounds can you deadlift?"

"What do you think of Coach K?"

"Is your family going to miss you if you move to North Carolina?"

"Why do you spend so much time by yourself in the weight room?"

The questions went on and on. Brian was not clearly not getting the message that I wasn't in the talking mood. I found myself getting angry. I was stressed about school and picking the right college, and Brian was making it worse.

I grabbed him by the front of his jersey and lifted him easily off the floor. I stared right into his scared eyes and screamed, "BRIAN! SHUT. UP. NOW. YOU ARE SO ANNOYING."

I unceremoniously dropped him, and he fell to the ground. My other teammates crowded around, laughing. "Ha! Brian, you got what was coming to you" they jeered. Brian had always been an easy target, but I had made him an acceptable one.

I watched the tears brim in Brian's eyes, and I saw my 5th grade self.

I could not write a book on friendship without writing about the toxicity of bullying.

My friends, I cannot begin to express the pain in my heart that bullying brings me. As a mental health professional, I feel twice as guilty for the behavior of my youth. When I began this book, I could not help but think of Brian and the suffering I caused him.

You see, bullying is not just about being a bully or being bullied.

It is about power.

When we assert power in our relationships we deny the survival of equality.

Since the dawn of upright humans, we have sought power over one another. The strongest among us were given food, safety, and respect.

Today, we continue to treat each other not as equals, but as opponents in the great human race. Romances turn abusive, coworkers create subterfuge and gossip, and moronic drivers change lanes without using their signal lights. In the pursuit of healthy and meaningful relationships, we must learn to reject the selfish allure of power.

Friendship, like any relationship, is vulnerable to imbalances of power. The perfect friendship is perfectly balanced, as all things should be. This chapter is all about learning to notice and address imbalances in your friendship.

Most power imbalances in relationships cause problems. The severity of those problems falls on a spectrum, ranging from assertive and passive to abusive and victimization. Although most friendships do not turn into bullying, many relationship dynamics can become problematic.

Let's break these power dynamics down into three main categories, in order from best to worst: **Egalitarian, Lessor and Greater,** and **Bullying and Bullied.**

The Healthiest Relationship: Egalitarian

Ideally, all friend relationships would be equal in power and respect. Egalitarian friendships are easily sustainable because both parties are invested and active in the relationship. A good example of egalitarian friendship can be seen among the heroes of *The Avengers*, where each hero is equally valued and involved. This is the dynamic all of us should strive to achieve.

Egalitarian friends see each other as peers, different but equal, and worthy of the relationship. Friends who enjoy egalitarian relationships feel that they both contribute to the relationship in comparable ways, which allows each to feel respected and valuable.

Here are some signs that your friendship is egalitarian:

- **Able to support one another.** The hallmark of all egalitarian friendships is high reciprocity; the process of giving one another equal shares of time, energy, and love. For example, if one friend experiences the death of a loved one, the other friend is available to comfort them and provide any needed support, and vice versa.

- **Trust in one another.** If one friend forgets their wallet while out on a lunch date, the other friend happily covers the cost of the meal knowing the favor will be returned. Or, when one friend hears a rumor about the other, they are more likely to side with their friend than believe what others say. This indicates vulnerability and closeness in the relationship.

- **Everyone's opinions matter.** If the friends must make a decision together, even something as small as what movie to watch, both are willing to consider one another's ideas. This indicates respect for the relationship.

- **Willingness to repair.** When rupture happens, both friends are willing to engage in a healing conversation to make amends and solve the problem. This demonstrates love, care, and desire to keep the relationship intact.

If your friendships are fairly egalitarian, congrats! Remember that no relationship is perfect, and you can always grow together as friends. Find ways to avoid stagnation by relying on the ten Friendship Fortifiers, and enjoy the ride.

The Imbalanced Relationship: The Lesser and the Greater

A lesser and greater friendship can feel great but is ultimately not sustainable. A positive example of this would be more like the hero and sidekick, like Batman and Robin; although, many look more like Dr. Frankenstein and Igor, where one friend is clearly dependent on or subservient to the other. Many of our relationships are naturally designed this way, such as that of a parent and a child.

Friendships between the lesser and the greater have a clear hierarchy. One friend is the cool one, the smart one, the rich one, and the other is their tag-along. The greater friend gets to feel superior or helpful, and the lesser friend gets to reap the benefits of relying on the other. Over time, imbalanced friendships like these can lead to problems, such as devaluation, power struggles, and loss of investment.

Here are a few signs that your friendship is imbalanced:

- **One friend is the support, the other is supported.** For example, one friend may be a constant source of emotional soothing, stabilization, and security for the other. Or, one may be overly needy and frequently seeking resources from their friends. This indicates that the relationship lacks reciprocity.

- **Mono-directional trust.** In other words, one is able to trust the other, but the other has little faith or trust in their friend. The trust only goes one way. You might be willing to let your friend drive your car, but they might not trust you to drive theirs. Although one friend might merely have trust issues, this can indicate a lack of willingness to be vulnerable or rely on one another.

- **One friend's opinion matters more.** If you want to watch *Star Wars* and they want to go to the beach, but your opinion matters more, then you probably aren't going to the beach. Or, one friend might always be "right" and the other is always "wrong." This can be a clear indication of who has the most power in the relationship.

- **Responsibility for rupture repair is not shared.** The power imbalance means that one friend needs the relationship more than the other. The lesser friend is often tasked with attempting the repair because they need the relationship. Imagine how stressful this can be for the lesser friend, particularly when they rely on the relationship for emotional or financial support.

If you find yourself in an imbalanced relationship, there are a few things you can do to even things out. First, try to identify ways for both friends to contribute equally. If one friend's needs are greater than the other, problem-solve to help them have their needs met through other sources. If one friend seems needless or defensive about relying on the other, have a conversation about how this affects the relationship.

Next, find opportunities for vulnerability and learned trust. Remember, friendship takes time to develop. Some relationships will start off imbalanced and grow to be more equal over time. Try to find time to learn more about one another, and be curious.

If time and mutual openness do not seem to help, try to communicate feelings of disrespect and devaluation in the relationship. Or, express feelings of being drained or feeling unsupported by your friend. This can sometimes create essential conflict in the relationship, allowing both friends to open up and find renewed understanding. Much like a bone that heals incorrectly, some issues require some breakage for healing to happen. Sometimes it can be useful to seek a third party to guide your conversation or to give you helpful advice for navigating the relationship.

Finally, if efforts to rebalance the relationship are unsuccessful, allow yourself permission to set boundaries with the relationship. Relational boundaries are barriers between you and the other person that you choose to put in place for your own sanity and wellbeing. Here are a few ideas for setting healthy boundaries:

- Limiting the amount of time and energy you devote to the relationship
- Restricting contact from the other person, such as:
  - Blocking them on social media
  - Turning off your cell phone at night
  - Only spend time with them on a particular weeknight
  - Moving out if you are living together
  - Setting a friendship budget and sticking to it
- Finding new friendships and spending more time with others

The Abusive Relationship: The Bully and the Bullied

A bully-bullied relationship can be incredibly toxic and is rarely sustainable. In *Harry Potter and the Chamber of Secrets*, this is Mr. Malfoy and Dobby. Abusive relationships like these are characterized by control: one partner is in control, the other is controlled.

Friendships - if I dare call them that - with abusive dynamics are designed to benefit the bully. The bully is able to feel powerful and safe by coercing the bullied into meeting their needs. The bullied are then put in a position of survival – better to permit the bully power than to face the consequences.

Here are some signs that the relationship might be abusive:

- **Control.** Relational terrorism. The bully is able to control the bullied through physical, emotional, or financial coercion. They threaten to cause harm or take away support when the bullied does something undesirable. Only one person in the relationship has power, leaving the other powerless. This demonstrates that this is not a friendship, this is ownership.

- **Lack of trust.** The bully does not trust the bullied, and vice versa. Rather than embodied by love and intimacy, the relationship is plagued with fear. The bully may monitor your location, your computer browser history, etc., to ensure their attachment with you is safe.

- **My way or the highway.** Another form of control, the bully has all authority over what happens in the relationship. The bullied have no opinion and no voice.

- **Rupture and deceptive repair.** Surprisingly, attempts at repair may exist in abusive relationships. The bully may bring apologetic gifts or say kind words after raging at the bullied. Sadly, these attempts are not true repair. Remember that repair requires a full understanding, amendment, and preventative problem-solving. The bully's apology is a deceptive way to maintain control by soothing strong emotions and maintaining the status quo.

If you find yourself in a truly abusive relationship, particularly those that are physically or emotionally unsafe, you must seek help. Although setting boundaries can sometimes be helpful, bullies might experience intense fear when you restrict their ability to monitor or control you. For free and confidential consultation, contact the National Domestic Violence Hotline at 1–800–799–7233. Make sure to call when you are in a safe place to talk freely and get the help you need.

You may also recognize that you have become controlling others. Many of us who engage in bullying behaviors do so because we are afraid, and we know what it is to be hurt. It doesn't have to be this way, you are not alone. Connect with a local counselor or psychologist to help you overcome the difficult dynamic of bullying and being bullied. You have the ability to find safety and normalcy again.

Chapter Summary

Every relationship has power. However, many relationships do not share the power equally. We find ourselves in relationships that are imbalanced, abusive even, and ultimately our desire for deep and meaningful friendship goes unmet. Learn to identify destructive dynamics in your relationships, and you can help keep good friendships from turning sour.

Questions to Ponder:

- What relationships do you most often find yourself in? Equal and respectful? Imbalanced and dependent? Abusive? Why is that?

- Who in your life can you trust to help you work through difficult power imbalances?

CHAPTER 15
YOUR FRIENDSHIP FORMULA

You have come far, my friends.

And now, you are ready to put it all together.

Look inward, and believe in yourself.

Take your newfound understanding of your unique needs and skills. Use a growth mindset, and pull the tooth to improve your capacity for friendship. As your health, sociability, and self-awareness increase, people will continue to feel more comfortable and drawn to the castle of your friendship.

Look outward, and discover new connections.

Learn to open yourself to friendship. Do not save seats at your table, bring more. Follow the dos and don'ts of relationship and, much like the hopeful gardener, you will notice your relationships blossom. And never, ever, forget to reach out to others.

Look in between, and enjoy the dance of friendship.

Notice what happens within the relationship, the shared product of two souls yearning for belonging. Find ways to notice subtle bids for connection, and respond with confidence to conflict and ruptures. Most importantly, recognize imbalances in your relationships, and pursue equality and growth together.

My heart soars at the hope that you will finally discover the warm embrace of friendship and belonging.

Please accept my deepest thanks for bringing my words into your adventure.

This book may end, but your journey towards friendship is only just beginning.

A FEW RESOURCES

Improving Your Social Fitness:

- www.improveyoursocialskills.com
- www.reddit.com/r/socialskills
- *Improve Your Social Skills* by Daniel Wendler
- *Level Up Your Social Life: The Gamer's Guide to Social Skills* by Daniel Wendler

Growing Your Physical Garden:

- *How to Boil Water* by Food Network Kitchens
- www.bodybuilding.com
- www.myfitnesspal.com
- www.benourished.com

Mastering Your Psychological Self

- www.psychologytoday.com
- *Hold Me Tight* by Sue Johnson
- *The Curse of the Self* by Mark Leary
- *I am Proud of You: Life Lessons from My Friend Fred Rogers* by Tim Madigan
- *Man's Search for Meaning* by Victor Frankl

- *The Four Most Important Things: A Book on Living* by Ira Byock

Orienting Your Spiritual Compass

- To the Moon, a video game by Kan Gao
- *Midnight Jesus* by Jamie Blaine
- *Beyond the Mirror* by Henri Nouwen
- *The Contented Soul* by Lisa McMinn
- *Tuesdays with Morrie* by Mitch Albom

REFERENCES

Ainsworth, M. D. S., Blehar, M. C., Waters, E., & Wall, S. N. (2015). *Patterns of attachment: A psychological study of the strange situation.* Psychology Press.

Bruch, E. E., & Newman, M. E. J. (2018). Aspirational pursuit of mates in online dating markets. *Science Advances, 4*(8), 9815.

Chapman, G. (2004). The five love languages: How to express heartfelt commitment to your mate. *Chicago, EL: Northfield Publishing.*

Hall, J. A. (2018). How many hours does it take to make a friend?. *Journal of social and personal relationships, 1, 19.*

Holt-Lunstad, J., Robles, T. F., & Sbarra, D. A. (2017). Advancing social connection as a public health priority in the United States. *American Psychologist, 72*(6), 517.

Holt-Lunstad, J., Smith, T. B., Baker, M., Harris, T., & Stephenson, D. (2015). Loneliness and social isolation as risk factors for mortality: a meta-analytic review. *Perspectives on Psychological Science, 10*(2), 227-237.

ABOUT THE AUTHOR

My name is Kyler, and I want to be your friend.

I am a (soon-to-be) Doctor of Clinical Psychology, and I specialize in pediatric and family mental health. I am also an author, public speaker, and advocate for marginalized communities.

My quest is to bring an end to the loneliness epidemic.

I love video games, fitness, and cooking (but mostly eating). I love my wife Mary more than anything else.

Please feel free reach out to me through my personal website: Kyler-Shumway.com

I love receiving emails from friends and readers. Let's get to know each other!

Made in the USA
Las Vegas, NV
05 September 2021

28153553R00100